G000099346

Christians in the Community of the Dome

The escalating challenges for Bible-believing Christians in Britain since the turn of the Millennium

Julian Mann

EP BOOKS

1st Floor Venture House, 6 Silver Court, Watchmead,
Welwyn Garden City, UK, AL7 1TS

www.epbooks.org
sales@epbooks.org

EP Books are distributed in the USA by:
JPL Distribution
3741 Linden Avenue Southeast
Grand Rapids, MI 49548

orders@jplbooks.com
www.jplbooks.com

© Julian Mann 2017.

British Library Cataloguing in Publication Data available

ISBN 978-1-78397-210-4

'In this book Julian Mann presents many disturbing case studies demonstrating the increasing legal pitfalls surrounding freedom of speech, religious freedom, homosexuality and gay rights and the resulting challenges which these pose to Christians today. He ends with a vision of what England might be like if a Bible based Christian revival took place.'

Dr Ben Kwashi, Archbishop of Jos Province,
Anglican Church of Nigeria

"This little book has provided us with an invaluable resource: we can often struggle to see the wood for the trees and the timelines in this book enable us to stand back and see the trajectories of recent years in our land. The book then moves on to speculate as to where these trajectories might lead in a number of scenarios for the future, helpfully mapped out by people whose observations I trust. They give grounds for hope as well as warnings of what may happen. Whether or not the scenarios prove accurate, it is wonderful to know that Jesus will build his church and the gates of hell will not prevail against it"

Andy Lines, Bishop in the Anglican Church in North America
(ACNA) with a Special Mission for Europe as supported by the
Archbishops of the Global Anglican Future Conference (GAFCON)

If you feel that sane Christian faith has been removed from the British shelves and replaced with bewildering alternatives, Julian Mann has kept a fascinating diary of the process this century. Interspersed with occasional interviews and finishing with the kind of renewal God is perfectly capable of, this is a brief book to inform, stir and strengthen.

Simon Manchester, Senior Minister, St Thomas'
Anglican Church North Sydney

This is a superb dystopian polemic in a proud English tradition, that of Swift and Orwell. The writer will not apologise for his fierce and uncompromising Christian faith and why should he? One feels reading these pages that if Christianity is once again to flourish in England it will need intellectual warriors of this hue and cast.

Michael Magarian QC, leading Criminal Defence Barrister.

Contents

Foreword

This book needs to be read. It won't take you long. It is fast-paced and in it Julian Mann prompts us to face up to the theological heresies of our time and to confront the cultural apostasy.

How should Christians relate to an increasingly de-Christianised public square where people are either ignorant of, or hostile toward, the worldview of the Bible? What are Christians to do when the Church is marginalised, sometimes heretical and the exclusive claims of the gospel are viewed as bigotry and the moral law in Scripture is seen as repressive and intolerant?

In this context Julian brilliantly summarises what many of us have lived through since the turn of the Millennium. He charts the times with searing clarity. In addressing the renewed encounter between biblical faith and the humanistic, Islamic, and pagan ideologies in our time, many Christians have decided to adopt overtly pluralistic or inclusivist perspectives. This book shows us how this is fatal.

Prophetic ministry begins by looking back in history and understanding where we have departed from God's word. True reformation in the Church in Britain will begin when we understand this and act differently.

Julian shows that the only hope in our times is found in Christ for culture. When Christians believe the promises of God's word, and act on their belief, our Lord Himself promises that they can remove mountains. When their faith is sterile and anorexic, they are ineffectual, and Satan in time gains wide dominance in the world (Matthew 17:14–21). That's a description of our culture and the one that Julian confronts us with.

Our perennial tendency is to live by sight, not by faith. It is to live in Satan's manufactured world, not God's actual world. Julian exposes this and exhorts us to our true calling to disciple the nation—not just individuals but our nation. This is our Great Commission and Cultural Mandate.

Let this book stir us to do the Lord's bidding and go out fearlessly to carry His witness to the world. Let's exchange the safety of inaction for the hazards of God-inspired progress. Invariably the power of God follows such action.

Cultural withdrawal and retrenchment will not keep the Church or the nation safe. The best defence is a good offence. Let's take Julian's challenge and rise to it.

Thank you Julian.

Andrea Minichiello Williams

Founder and CEO, Christian Concern & the Christian Legal Centre Andrea qualified as a barrister in 1988 and has practised at all levels of the British judicial system. She pioneered the Student and Policy work of the Lawyers Christian Fellowship, and went on to found Christian Concern and the Christian Legal Centre, which have run some of the most high profile Christian freedom cases and campaigns in Europe. She is a leading analyst, campaigner, and spokeswoman on issues of national importance in the moral life of the nation and as  defender of Christian liberties in the parliamentary process, the justice system and the media. Andrea is married and mother to four children.

To my wife Lisa—Proverbs 31:29–31

I

The Community of the Dome

And they said, Go to, let us build us a city and a tower, whose top may reach unto heaven: and let us make us a name, lest we be scattered abroad upon the face of the whole earth (Genesis 11:4).

This book is about the changing social and political climate for Bible-believing Christians in Britain since the turn of the Millennium. In the year 2000, Tony Blair was Prime Minister having led the Labour Party, which he had rebranded New Labour, to a decisive General Election victory in 1997. His government built a dome in Greenwich, south-east London, in which it held a Millennium celebration on New Year's Eve in 1999.

After New Labour's second decisive election victory in 2001, I began to sense that the attitude of the political class in our country was changing from a broad acceptance of Britain's Christian heritage to hostile indifference. Had I paid better attention, I might have realised earlier that New Labour's core aim of 'modernising'[1] the country inevitably

---

1 In his foreword to the 1997 Labour election manifesto, Tony Blair had written: 'We have modernised the Labour Party and we will modernise Britain. This

entailed clashes with biblical Christianity because this faith had been so important in shaping Britain's past.

After becoming a Church of England vicar with pastoral responsibility for a local church in 2000, I was also noticing that a growing culture of political correctness was putting pressure on Christian people not to speak of certain essential biblical truths, such as Jesus being the only way to God and heterosexual marriage being the only right context for the expression of sexual love.

Noticeable too in the wider culture was a growing tendency to narcissism and self-worship with state schools seeming to promote this ethos among children and young people. This culture seemed to be connected with the tendency in church services to shorten prayers of confession—'confession lite' one might call it—or even to omit prayers of confession altogether. It also seemed to be connected with a growing tendency to self-censorship among some Christians who would describe themselves as biblically orthodox over such vital doctrines as the sinfulness of humanity and the judgement of God.

I tried to express my feeling about the changing spiritual atmosphere in a short story, which I have updated a little. Some readers may consider that I should have stuck to the day job but here is *The Community of the Dome*:

---

means knowing where we want to go; being clear-headed about the country's future; telling the truth; making tough choices; insisting that all parts of the public sector live within their means; taking on vested interests that hold people back; standing up to unreasonable demands from any quarter; and being prepared to give a moral lead where government has responsibilities it should not avoid' (http://www.politicsresources.net/area/uk/man/lab97.htm).

The Dome squatted in the rain as Peter entered the Media-zone for his last seminar before the Winterval vacation. Peter was a student at the Dome Academy, an elite feeder for both the Modernisation Commission and the People's Media.

For festival time, he went to his parents' home in a check-pointed and well-guarded garden suburb. Though the married family was intentionally disparaged as an outdated, repressive relic of the past across the modernised zones, it remained popular among the metropolitan elite. With a married father and mother, Peter belonged to a tiny fraction of the population. It was in the pocket of a borrowed suit that Peter found the book. He had been invited to a 1960s retro party and his father had said he could borrow an old Mod suit belonging to his grandfather up in the attic.

'To Pete—this'll really blow your mind. Love, Zoe' was written on the inside cover of the paperback, which was in good condition but bearing the desiccated pages associated with its age. Peter noticed some strange markings on the back—2/- net in U.K. The front-cover pictured a large golden lion and a boy wearing shorts. Its title: *The Lion, the Witch and the Wardrobe* by C.S. Lewis.

Peter had liked his granddad, and was curious about the book. He read it from cover to cover and found its imagery compelling—the strange land entered through the wardrobe, the perpetual winter, the Witch and her secret police, and above all the towering figure of the Lion.

But he was baffled by other aspects of the tale, particularly the events surrounding the death of the Lion. What on earth had the boy Edmund done wrong? What was wrong with disclosing his enemies' whereabouts to the Witch? What was wrong with wanting to gain promotion for yourself at the expense of others?

He could not understand the reason for the gory and humiliating Voluntary Self-Euthanasia of the Lion. It was not as if he was seeking to avoid pain, inconvenience, or shame for himself. He was sacrificing himself for somebody else. It seemed folly to Peter.

Voluntary Self-Euthanasia

At the beginning of the Guevara term after the Winterval break, Terry, also a student at the Dome Academy and a friend of Peter, began to suffer persistent headaches. He presented himself to one of the Dome's in-house healing enhancers in the Detox-zone. The tests began, the operation occurred, the ensuing therapy continued, but the brain tumour was terminal.

Voluntary Self-Euthanasia had been introduced by the Commission to deal with the growing problem of an ageing population. It was also useful in depleting the burgeoning prison population amongst the underclass.

The framers of the legislation considered that the growing culture of shame surrounding death would lead most terminal patients to sign their own VSE consent forms. But if the patient was too incapacitated to give their own consent, VSE procedure allowed the obtaining of a signature of consent from the stakeholder's employer. For educational institutions, the Chair of Enablers' signature was required; for retired persons, the Commissioner for Pensions was responsible for issuing VSE signatures.

Early on in the scheme, a legal challenge by the relative of an elderly VSE patient on grounds of age discrimination had ensured that regulations had to be applied in an egalitarian manner across all age groups. VSE age discrimination was ruled contrary to human rights.

When the system first began procedures were observed carefully due to the threat of legal challenges and the initial political opposition to VSE. Initially, the signatures of two healing enhancers were required to verify that the patient was unable to give consent before the main signatory could give theirs and VSE proceed. There was also an appeals procedure for relatives, which did in some cases delay VSE.

But now the system was operating in a streamlined, and uncharacteristically for the times, unbureaucratic manner. The main signatory would generally be satisfied with one healing enhancer's signature and VSE could proceed speedily.

Terry knew his moment would come as soon as the sun-tanned Chair of Enablers took his case in hand and issued the necessary decree. Confined to the Detox-zone, he asked for and obtained permission to visit the Spirituality-zone.

Banks of computer screens lined the Spirituality-zone. Aromas filled the air and the atmosphere was enhanced by electric candelabra projecting soft lights.

Terry keyed in his password.

HELLO TERRY. WELCOME TO THE SPIRITUALITY-ZONE. YOU ARE INVITED TO CREATE YOUR OWN IMAGE.

Since childhood, Terry had particularly liked cats.

I WOULD LIKE A CAT.

One duly appeared on the screen, sitting upright and staring benevolently.

WHAT WOULD YOU LIKE TO SAY TO THE CAT, TERRY?

I AM A CANDIDATE FOR VSE. WHAT GUIDANCE CAN YOU OFFER ME?

REMEMBER THERE'S ONLY ONE YOU, TERRY. YOU'RE VERY SPECIAL.

When the decree came from the Lennon-zone, Terry's VSE was performed by a petite healing enhancer who gave him a massage and waved a crystal over his prostrate body before administering the injection. Terry breathed his last and was instantly cremated. His ashes were placed in a container shaped like an old-fashioned Oscar. Peter attended the ceremony admitting Terry's avatar into the Dome Academy's Hall of Fame.

The Community of the Dome gathered in the Nietzsche Hall on a summer's day at the end of the McGuinness term for its annual Media Idol. The competition was judged by a panel of People's Celebrities. Each contestant was tasked to deliver a policy announcement at a Commission press briefing, speaking into an autocue with their face projected onto a large screen behind them.

For the first round, contestants briefed the media on new funding for 24-hour nurseries on the day that a commissioner had been charged with obstructing the course of a VSE authorisation. For the second, they were tasked to humiliate an unmodernised journalist with an impersonation of a personal mannerism.

Peter's punchy performances in all the rounds won him the prize and in the blaze of a simulated firework display he was declared Dome Media Idol of the Year. The Community of the Dome then linked arms and sang the People's Anthem, Imagine. On this occasion, Peter's lips did not move. His mind was elsewhere.

———————————➤●◀———————————

Though Tony Blair's New Labour won by a thumping majority in 1997 of 179 seats in the House of Commons, it was socially cautious in its first administration after 18 years of Conservative rule. New Labour's celebrations of the turn of the Millennium in the infamous Greenwich Dome even featured the then Archbishop of Canterbury, George Carey, leading Christian prayers amid the popular music acts.

New Labour did effect a significant change to public morals in the fourth year of its first term. In November 2000, it over-ruled the House of Lords and lowered the age of consent for homosexual relations between males from 18 to 16. This meant that a male in his 40s could legally have sex with a boy who might not yet have completed his development into puberty, provided he was not the boy's teacher or in some other 'position of trust.'

But the legislative evidence points to the fact that New Labour's radical agenda of social change and its assault on the post-1960s vestiges of Christian Britain became incarnate after its second victory over the Conservatives in 2001. Moreover, after New Labour left office in 2010, its social trajectory demonstrably continued under a Conservative Prime Minister, David Cameron. So, this story of the escalating challenges facing Bible-believing Christians in Britain in the new Millennium begins in AD 2001.

2

Timelines of the Falling Temperature

Thrice was I beaten with rods, once I was stoned, thrice I suffered shipwreck, a night and a day I have been in the deep (2 Corinthians 11:25).

Before we go back to 2001, it is important to register that this account is not meant to be a victim narrative. Compared to the situation of first-century Christians such as the Apostle Paul, quoted above, and of many Christians around the world today, we British Christians enjoy substantial legal protections.

But when in 2009 the then Bishop of Winchester, the late Michael Scott Joynt (1943–2014), wrote, 'The sad fact is that Britain—which owes so much to its Christian heritage—is increasingly becoming a 'cold' place for Christians,' he surely conjured up a powerful image.[1] Whilst the atmosphere for Christians in the UK is still well above freezing point, the temperature has been noticeably falling.

---

1   In a foreword to a report by Christian Action Research and Education (CARE) on the potential impact of the Equality Bill then going through Parliament.

The plan here is to produce four timelines concurrent with the periods between General Elections since 2001, with some concluding items in the aftermath of the June 2017 General Election. These timelines aim to chronicle political developments and cases affecting orthodox Christians, particularly when they have been seeking to uphold their beliefs in secular employment and in public proclamation. For reasons of space and readability, the timelines cannot be fully comprehensive, but the Lord willing they will give a sense of the falling temperature.

After the second timeline there is an interview. *Mail on Sunday* columnist Peter Hitchens reflects on the socially radical heart of the New Labour project and on the threat to Christian freedom of expression from political correctness.

Two evangelical Christian organisations feature prominently in this account, the Christian Institute and Christian Concern. A word of introduction is important about each. Based in Newcastle and founded in 1991 by church leaders and professionals, the Christian Institute is a charity which according to its website is 'committed to upholding the truths of the Bible.' Through its Legal Defence Fund, it has supported many of the Christians mentioned in this book.

Based in central London and founded in 2008 by lawyers, Christian Concern is a not-for-profit company. According to its website, it cannot register as a charity because of its campaigning activities, but it is reliant on voluntary donations. It works 'to infuse a biblical worldview into every aspect of society' and aims 'to be a strong Christian voice in the public sphere, arguing passionately for the truth of the gospel and defending the historic freedoms that we have enjoyed in this nation for so long.'

Its sister organisation, the Christian Legal Centre, defends a 'wide variety of individuals and churches who have suffered discrimination and challenges because of their desire to live and work according to biblical beliefs.'

This book concludes with three imaginary scenarios for Britain in 2050.

First, there is an account by a fictional British Christian woman living under dominant Islam. Then in a two-part interview Andrew Symes, executive secretary of the international orthodox Anglican network and information resource, Anglican Mainstream, imagines himself as a Christian leader in a totally secular state in which public religion is banned. Finally, I imagine myself as a surprised 86-year-old retired clergyman during a Christian revival in 2050.

None of these scenarios is a dogmatic prediction; they are rather an attempt to stimulate the reader's own imaginative thinking about the spiritual, moral and social trends signalled in the timelines.

But for now back to 2001.

3
First Timeline 2001–2005

Thou shalt have none other gods before me. Thou shalt not make thee any graven image, or any likeness of any thing that is in heaven above, or that is in the earth beneath, or that is in the waters beneath the earth (Deuteronomy 5:7–8).

2001

June: New Labour under Tony Blair won the General Election with a majority of 166 seats in the House of Commons. No Labour government in the twentieth-century had won such a majority for a second term. In his victory speech Mr Blair said: 'I have just returned from Buckingham Palace, from my audience with the Queen. I want to say what an enormous privilege and honour it is to be trusted with the government of this country... Finally, in respect of Europe and the wider world, we need to make changes there too so that we are engaged, exerting influence, having the self belief not to turn our back on the world or retreat into isolationism,' *The Guardian* reported.

September: Following the resignation of William Hague, Iain Duncan Smith, the MP for Chingford and Woodford Green, was elected leader of the Conservative Party and thus leader of Her Majesty's Most Loyal Opposition. Mr Duncan Smith was the first Roman Catholic to lead the Conservative Party. A former soldier, he had served as Shadow Secretary of State for Defence from 1999–2001.

October: Police arrested a 69-year-old evangelical street preacher in Bournemouth town centre and charged him with harassment under Section 5 of the Public Order Act 1986. Harry Hammond, who suffered from Asperger's Syndrome, had been bearing a placard that read: 'Jesus is alive. Stop immorality, stop homosexuality, stop lesbianism.' He was confronted by a 40-strong crowd, pelted with mud and water and knocked to the ground. As the Christian Institute later described the incident: 'Two police officers arrived and, amazingly, arrested Mr Hammond.'[1]

November: New Labour tried to introduce a criminal offence of 'incitement to religious hatred' in its Anti-Terrorism, Crime and Security Bill.

December: The government was forced to drop the move after two defeats in the House of Lords. But the idea that the State should regulate religious debate was to rear its head again.

---

1   *Salt and Light, Christian Institute Annual Review 2001–2002*, p15. There are different reports about the precise wording on the late Harry Hammond's banner. In its 2008 booklet, The 'homophobic hatred offence,' free speech and religious liberty, the *Christian Institute* cited the wording as 'Stop immorality,' 'Stop Homosexuality,' 'Stop Lesbianism,' Jesus is Lord' (p11). Whilst orthodox Christians can rejoice in the truth of both 'Jesus is alive' and 'Jesus is Lord,' the balance of probability on the placard leans towards 'Jesus is Lord,' in addition to the statements about homosexuality. Discussing the case on the Free Speech Debate website, journalist and author Timothy Garton Ash reported that the words 'Jesus is Lord' were inscribed on each corner of the banner.

2002

January: Homosexual campaign group Stonewall was able to bring its activism nearer the heart of government. With its assistance, Liberal Democrat peer Lord Lester of Herne Hill introduced a Civil Partnerships Bill in the House of Lords, which aimed to create a status equivalent to marriage for homosexual couples who had lived together for six months. Lord Lester withdrew his private member's bill after its Second Reading in order to allow the government to set up a team of civil servants to prepare the way for the legal recognition of same-sex couples.

April: Harry Hammond was convicted of harassment and fined £300, plus £395 costs, by Wimborne magistrates' court. The Christian Institute set up a fighting fund to assist his appeal.

August: Harry Hammond died. His supporters resolved to continue his case in the public interest.

October: At the Conservative conference in Bournemouth, new party chairman Theresa May, MP for Maidenhead, told delegates: 'Yes, we've made progress, but let's not kid ourselves. There's a way to go before we can return to government. There's a lot we need to do in this party of ours. Our base is too narrow and so, occasionally, are our sympathies. You know what some people call us: the nasty party,' *The Guardian* reported.

November: The House of Commons over-ruled the House of Lords and passed the Adoption and Children Act allowing homosexual and heterosexual cohabiting couples to adopt children jointly. Previously, adoption had been restricted to single people and heterosexually married couples. The change came into force in 2005.

2003

March: The United States of America and Britain invaded Iraq. Mr Blair told the House of Commons that the reason for military action was that Iraq had weapons of mass destruction which were a threat to British national security.

June: The American magazine, *Vanity Fair*, published an interview with Tony Blair in which his director of communications and strategy, Alastair Campbell, was reported as saying: 'We don't do God.' In the piece, 'Blair's Big Gamble,' writer David Margolick described the incident as follows: 'As he always does, Alastair Campbell, the former London newsman who is Blair's director of communications, political strategist, and protector, hovers nearby, ostensibly involved in a separate conversation. But when the topic turns to religion, his ever sensitive antennae home in. Campbell, who worships a soccer team more than any church, has never forgotten the 1996 article (in which Mr Blair, then Leader of the Opposition, wrote about his faith) and how it was construed to mean that Tories were too selfish to be good Christians. Ever since, he has tried to steer Blair clear of the topic. 'Is he on to God?' Campbell asks Blair—the 'he' being me. 'We don't do God,' Campbell declares. 'I'm sorry. We don't do God.'

Parliament implemented an EU employment directive outlawing discrimination on the grounds of sexual orientation in the workplace. The government inserted an amendment allowing religious organisations to refuse to employ a non-believer or to dismiss an employee who abandoned their faith. The BBC reported: 'The gay-rights campaigning group, Stonewall, was angry and astonished at the amendment. Its parliamentary director, Sasha Deshmukh, blames pressure on the government from evangelicals within the Church of England.'

November: New Labour, with the support of Conservative 'modernisers,' repealed Section 28 of the Local Government Act 1988, which had forbidden the promotion of homosexuality in maintained schools. The government had tried to abolish Section 28 in 2000 but had been defeated in the Lords. The Scottish Parliament had abolished the provision in 2000 but now teachers gained licence to promote homosexual relationships in schools in England, Wales and Northern Ireland.

December: US forces discovered Iraq's dictator, Saddam Hussein, hiding in Tikrit. He was executed by the new Iraqi government in 2006.

2004

January: The High Court in London ruled that the late Harry Hammond had been 'properly convicted' by Wimborne magistrates. *The Daily Telegraph* reported: 'Lord Justice May, sitting with Mr Justice Harrison, said it had been open to magistrates in Wimborne, Dorset, to convict Mr Hammond in April 2002. Mr Hammond's behaviour "went beyond legitimate protest". Executors of Mr Hammond's estate brought the appeal in an attempt to clear his name.'

February: Former Home Secretary Michael Howard, who had replaced Iain Duncan Smith as leader of the Conservative Party in November 2003, spoke at the Policy

Exchange explaining his support for New Labour's plan for civil partnerships. *The Guardian* carried the full text of his speech. Mr Howard said: 'To recognise civil partnerships is not, in any way, to denigrate or downgrade marriage. It is to recognise and respect the fact that many people want to live their lives in different ways. And it is not the job of the State to put barriers in their way.' The paper commented: 'Although his declaration may confound some Conservatives, the timing of the speech—delivered to Francis Maude's centre-right thinktank, Policy Exchange—indicates a rapprochement with the socially liberal, so-called "Portillista" wing of the party.'[1]

November: Parliament passed the Civil Partnerships Act, giving homosexual couples in England and Wales the same legal rights as husbands and wives.

2005

March: The BBC Governors' programme complaints committee gave its ruling on *Jerry Springer—the Opera*, a so-called comedy broadcast by BBC 2 in January in which, apart from other blasphemies about Jesus which will not be repeated here, 'obscene language was put into the mouths of members of the Holy Family.' The committee reported: 'By a majority of four to one, the complaints (around 60,000 of them) were not upheld. The Committee's finding was that BBC management's decision to broadcast *Jerry Springer—the*

---

1   Portillista' (pronounced Portiyeesta) was the Spanish-sounding nickname for the socially liberal Tory tendency associated with the former Conservative Defence Secretary and subsequent TV personality, Michael Portillo. Francis Maude was another prominent Conservative 'moderniser' who after the May 2005 General Election became Chairman of the Conservative Party.

Opera was not in breach of the relevant editorial standards, codes and guidelines.'[1]

April: The US Criminal Intelligence Agency (CIA) issued a report declaring that no weapons of mass destruction had been found in Iraq. Tony Blair called the General Election for May 5th.

---

[1] http://www.bbc.co.uk/complaints/pdf/appsspringer.pdf

4

Second Timeline 2005–2010

The mighty God, even the Lord, hath spoken, and called the earth from the rising of the sun unto the going down thereof. Out of Zion, the perfection of beauty, God hath shined (Psalm 50:1–2).

2005 continuing

May: In the General Election, the Labour Party led by Tony Blair won a third term of office by a majority of 66 seats in the House of Commons. This was the first time in British history that Labour had won three General Elections in a row. Mr Blair told party activists in his Sedgefield constituency: 'I know too that Iraq has been a divisive issue in this country but I hope now that we can unite again and look to the future—there and here,' the BBC reported.

June: In line with its election manifesto, New Labour published the Religious and Racial Hatred Bill. This aimed to extend offences on incitement to racial hatred under the 1986 Public Order Act to cover the stirring up of hatred against people of any religious faith. The offence, which was to be determined by the perception of the alleged victim, would carry a maximum seven-year jail sentence. *The*

Guardian reported: 'The government argues the present law is unsatisfactory because it covers followers of some faiths, such as Jews and Sikhs who are also considered as racial groups, while giving no protection to Muslims, who come from many racial backgrounds.'

August: In its campaign against the proposed incitement to religious hatred offence, the Christian Institute organised a series of meetings addressed by Australian pastor Daniel Scot. It later explained: 'Pastor Scot was convicted of a similar offence in Australia for having calmly stated mainstream Christian views on Islam. His case was a perfect example of the kind of injustices that can result from "religious hatred" laws.'[1]

October: The House of Lords voted to amend the Racial and Religious Hatred Bill. The offence of religious hatred would only include threatening words or behaviour which were intended to stir up hatred. The Lords also inserted protections for free speech and evangelism. In June, comedian Rowan Atkinson had called the unamended Bill 'draconian' and 'a sledgehammer to crack a nut,' the BBC reported.

December: At the age of 39, David Cameron, MP for Witney in Oxfordshire, was elected leader of the Conservative Party. BBC political editor Nick Robinson said Mr Cameron's victory indicated that the Conservatives were 'coming to terms with Tony Blair.' The BBC also reported that at a dinner party with newspaper executives on the eve of his leadership pitch to the Conservative conference in October, Mr Cameron had declared: 'I am the heir to Blair.' Before entering Parliament in 2001, Mr Cameron had been director of corporate affairs for a television company.

---

1 'Pray for those in authority' *The Christian Institute Annual Review 2005–2006*, p6

2006

January: London's *Evening Standard* reported that leaders of the Gay Police Association (GPA) had made a formal complaint to Metropolitan Police chiefs 'demanding that they bar members of the Christian Police Association from the force as they do members of the BNP,' referring to the neofascist British National Party. Thus, an association of some British police officers promoted the idea that the orthodox Christian view on human sexuality, held by people from diverse racial and cultural backgrounds, should be put on a par with racial hatred.

February: The Lords' amendments to the religious hatred measure were upheld by the House of Commons against the government's wishes. The *Independent* reported: 'Records showed that Mr Blair voted in the first of two divisions on Lords amendments to the Bill, only to see the Government lose by 288 to 278, a majority of 10. But Mr Blair failed to vote in a second division when MPs voted by 283 votes to 282, majority one, to back safeguards inserted by peers.'

June: Strathclyde Fire Service took disciplinary action against nine firemen in Glasgow, five of whom were Roman Catholic, for refusing to participate in a gay pride march. Brian Herbert, the Watch Manager of the unit, was demoted and had his salary cut by £5,000. Mr Herbert and his colleagues were also ordered to undergo intense 'diversity' training. The Christian Institute paid for a barrister to advise Mr Herbert, who appealed using internal disciplinary procedures. As a result Mr Herbert was later restored to his original salary and rank.

October: The Advertising Standards Authority (ASA) ruled that an advertisement placed by the GPA in the

'Diversity' section of *The Independent* in June, headed 'in the name of the father,' was untruthful. The advert claimed: 'In the last 12 months, the GPA has recorded a 74% increase in homophobic incidents, where the sole or primary motivating factor was the religious belief of the perpetrator.' The BBC reported an ASA spokeswoman as saying: 'This is our most complained about campaign advert of the year so far. People thought it was portraying Christians in a bad light.'

2007

January: Carlisle Council told an Open Air Mission (OAM) evangelist that he could not distribute Christian leaflets in public without a licence. It transpired that the council had failed to note that the Clean Neighbourhoods and Environment Act 2005, which gave power to local authorities to control distribution of free literature in town centres, specifically exempted religious literature. The Christian Institute helped OAM draft a letter of complaint, pointing out the misapplication of the law.

February: Carlisle Council accepted they had unlawfully interfered with the evangelist's right to distribute free religious literature in public.

April: The Equality Act (Sexual Orientation) Regulations 2007 came into force. These regulations outlawed discrimination on the grounds of sexual orientation in the provision of goods, facilities, services, education and public functions. Roman Catholic adoption agencies who out of religious conviction were only prepared to place children with heterosexually married couples faced the choice between moral compromise and closure. These regulations were also to have a significant impact on Christian bed and breakfast and small business owners.

May: Tony Blair announced that he was to step down as Prime Minister on June 27th after ten years in the role. US President Bush said: 'When Tony Blair tells you something— as we say in Texas—you can take it to the bank. He's a political figure capable of thinking over the horizon. He's a long-term thinker,' *The Guardian* reported.

June: MPs gave Tony Blair a standing ovation at his final Prime Minister's Questions in the House of Commons. Television footage showed David Cameron cheer-leading Conservative MPs, waving his arm to indicate that he expected all of them to join in with the applause.

The Chancellor of the Exchequer, Gordon Brown, MP for Kirkcaldy and Cowdenbeath, who on June 24th had become leader of the Labour Party, took over as Prime Minister.

October: National Churchwatch, sponsored by Ecclesiastical Insurance to provide safety advice for churches and church workers, warned vicars to take off their dog collars when on their own. In a survey of 90 London clergy which the group carried out in 2006, nearly half said they had been attacked in the past twelve months. According to *The Daily Telegraph*, Nick Tolson, the coordinator of National Churchwatch, said clergy 'haven't been streetwise in the past. They need to realise that wearing the dog collar makes them a target, especially in the case of single females. It isn't wise for them to wear it out shopping or in the car and they should never wear it when alone. The Archbishop and other bishops should give a lead in this.'

2008

February: In Birmingham, a police community support officer told two church workers: 'You can't preach here, this is a Muslim area.' The officer also told them: 'You have been warned. If you come back here and get beat up, well you have been warned.' After the two Christians made a formal complaint, West Midlands Police said: 'There are not any no-go areas in the West Midlands Police area.'[1]

April: In the House of Lords, the late David Waddington (1929–2017), a Conservative peer who had served as Home Secretary in the government led by Margaret Thatcher in the 1980s, successfully inserted a free speech defence in New Labour's proposed law against homophobic hatred. The Criminal Justice and Immigration Bill sought to introduce an offence of 'incitement to homophobic hatred,' carrying a maximum seven-year prison sentence. The so-called Waddington amendment allowed for the criticism of sexual conduct. It declared: 'Nothing in this Part (i.e. the section of the Bill relating to homophobic hatred) shall be read or given effect in a way which prohibits or restricts discussion of, criticism of or expressions of antipathy towards, conduct relating to a particular sexual orientation, or urging persons of a particular sexual orientation to refrain from or modify conduct related to that orientation.'[2]

July: The late Lillian Ladele (1960–2015), who as a serving London marriage registrar had told Islington Council that she could not in Christian conscience register civil

---

1   *Marginalising Christians—Instances of Christians being sidelined in modern Britain*, The Christian Institute, 2009, p37.

2   *The 'homophobic hatred offence,' free speech and religious liberty*, The Christian Institute, 2008, p38.

partnerships, won an employment tribunal case against her employer. In 2007, a council disciplinary panel had threatened her with the sack if she continued to refuse to officiate at civil partnership ceremonies. The tribunal ruled that Miss Ladele had been discriminated against on grounds of religious beliefs and harassed.

September: US-based global bank, Lehman Brothers, collapsed sparking an international credit crunch. This had the effect of deepening the recession into which the British economy had already dipped in the April-June 2008 quarter.

December: Islington Council succeeded in getting July's ruling in favour of Lillian Ladele overturned in the Employment Appeal Tribunal. Miss Ladele signalled her intent to take the case to the Court of Appeal.

2009

January: The government announced its intention to use the Coroners and Justice Bill to overturn the Waddington free speech amendment to the Criminal Justice and Immigration Act 2008, which had introduced an offence of incitement to homophobic hatred.

July: Conservative leader David Cameron apologised for the Thatcher government's introduction of Section 28, which had prohibited the promotion of homosexuality in schools (see November 2003). Speaking at a gay pride event, Mr Cameron said: 'I am sorry for Section 28. We got it wrong. It was an emotional issue. I hope you can forgive us,' *The Daily Telegraph* reported. The first Tory leader to speak at a gay pride event, Mr Cameron was also reported as saying: 'It is remarkable to have a Conservative leader standing on a gay pride platform. Five years ago not many gays would have turned up. Five years ago not many Tories would have turned up either.'

Lord Dear, a former chief constable and inspector of constabulary, argued in the House of Lords that the Waddington clause was helping the police. The *Independent* reported him telling peers: 'Prior to this House approving the Waddington amendment a year ago, the police regularly received complaints from homosexual groups that exception was taken to remarks that homosexuality was deplored on religious grounds. They were forced to act. With the Waddington amendment the police are released from a virtual strait-jacket that was imposed on them before. They can exercise common sense and good judgment on the day and they can police with a light touch.'

November: The government conceded parliamentary defeat in its bid to remove the Waddington amendment from its homophobic hatred law.

The BBC reported: 'MPs have voted four times to scrap it but it has been repeatedly overturned in the Lords, who again last night (November 11th) voted by 179 to 135 to keep it.' Lord Waddington had told peers: 'If we are to finish up with a free speech clause in the religious hatred offence but no free speech clause here, we're simply asking for trouble.'

December: Lilian Ladele lost her case for religious discrimination at the Court of Appeal. She signalled her intention to appeal to the Supreme Court of the United Kingdom of Great Britain and Northern Ireland. The *Daily Mail* reported: 'The landmark case was the most important legal test yet in the struggle between Christians and the gay rights lobby. Lord Neuberger, sitting with two other senior judges, said Labour's 2007 *Sexual Orientation Regulations*—which make it illegal to refuse to serve someone on grounds of their sexual orientation—trump the rights of religious believers.'

2010

March: The Supreme Court refused to give Lillian Ladele permission to appeal. She signalled the possibility of taking her case to the European Court of Human Rights.

April: Shadow Home Secretary Chris Grayling, Conservative MP for Epsom and Ewell, hit a media firestorm after *The Observer* published a recording of him saying during a Q&A at the Centre for Policy Studies:

> I think we need to allow people to have their own consciences ... If you look at the case of 'Should a Christian hotel owner have the right to exclude a gay couple from their hotel?' I took the view that if it's a question of somebody who's doing a B&B in their own home, that individual should have the right to decide who does and who doesn't come into their own home. If they are running a hotel on the High Street, I really don't think that it is right in this day and age that a gay couple should walk into a hotel and be turned away because they are a gay couple, and I think that is where the dividing line comes.

He later apologised for giving 'the wrong impression,' insisting he was fully supportive of gay rights, *The Guardian* reported.

New Labour's Equality Bill passed into law. In its 2010 annual review, 'Seek the peace of the city' (p4), the Christian Institute reported that 'the passage of the Bill gave Christians the opportunity to raise concerns about how 'equality and diversity' rules have been used to push Christians out of public life. The plight of religious adoption agencies (see April 2007) was regularly cited. Almost all such agencies have been shut down or forced to abandon their religious ethos because of sexual orientation laws that fail to protect liberty of conscience.'

Prime Minister Gordon Brown called the General Election for May 6th.

5

The Socially Radical
Heart of New Labour

To whom then will ye liken me, or shall I be equal? saith the Holy One (Isaiah 40:25).

Peter Hitchens was born in 1951, the son of a Royal Navy Commander who served in the Arctic Convoys during World War II. He was a political and foreign correspondent for *The Daily Express* from 1977 to 2000 when he became a columnist for *The Mail on Sunday*. A former atheist, he is now a practising Anglican Christian. His celebrated book, *The Rage Against God*, was published in 2010. Here, he answers some questions from the author.

Why were you able to discern early on the direction New Labour was going to take?

Because, as a former Marxist and a former member of the Labour Party, I understand the codes in which politics is nowadays discussed. Even before the collapse of the USSR and the end of the Cold War, the Western left had abandoned old-fashioned Leninism (seize the barracks, the post office and the railway station), and chosen instead

Gramsci's plan[1]—cultural hegemony first, then the rest will follow. I also knew from friends in New Labour that they regarded their 'project' as an enormous revolutionary change. The burden of these private conversations was interestingly confirmed by the former Blair aide Peter Hyman, writing in *The Observer* on 20th December 2015:

> New Labour sought political hegemony: winning power and locking out the Tories to ensure that the 21st century was a Labour century with Labour values in contrast to a Tory-dominated 20th century. The scale of that ambition, in a country dominated by a stridently rightwing press and the quiet conservatism of large swaths of the British people, was breathtaking. If Labour could be in power for a serious amount of time, then the country would, we believed, change for good; not a burst of socialism for one time (if that), but changed institutions and values that could shape the country for all time.

What is political correctness?

The use of policed language and speech codes to impose a code of beliefs, largely on sexual politics, on the whole culture. Its great strength is that its apparent target is the stupid and coarse insults once shamefully directed against certain people, which it effectively stamps out. Who can disapprove of that? Not I, for one. The problem is that it also stamps out any neutral expressions, which are now regarded as insufficiently

---

1   Antonio Gramsci (1891–1937), a founder of the Italian Communist Party, imprisoned by the Italian fascist dictator Benito Mussolini in 1926: 'Extracts of Gramsci's prison writings were published for the first time in the mid-20th century; the complete *Quaderni del carcere* (Prison Notebooks) appeared in 1975. Many of his propositions became a fundamental part of Western Marxist thought and influenced the post-World War II strategies of communist parties in the West' (https://www.britannica.com/biography/Antonio-Gramsci).

approving of the sexual revolution, or of multiculturalism in general. As a result it becomes an engine of the thought police, who can both identify and attack anyone insufficiently keen on these developments.

In June 2002 you wrote a letter to The Spectator *in support of Harry Hammond's legal fund. Why were you so concerned about what happened to him?*

As I explained in the article [please see the extract from Mr Hitchens's May 2002 *Spectator* article below his answer] because the police and courts had intervened on the side of radical speech codes, instead of maintaining a proper neutrality over the exercise of free speech.

If condemnation of an action is deemed to be insulting to anyone who does that action, then almost all absolute morality is outlawed. Those who write about such issues, as I do, often receive censorious letters claiming that our articles have insulted the writer. No matter that we have never heard of this individual and have made a general statement about unmarried mothers, employment quotas, homosexuality or whatever it is. These sensitive people have all taken it personally. This conveniently means that they do not have to argue their case. It also means that a legitimate opinion about a type of behaviour is magically transmuted into so-called hate-speech, so offensive to certain persons that it is likely to provoke them to fury. The implication is that it ought not to have been said or written. Such attitudes are already in power on most British university campuses, where the sexual-liberation lobby has almost completely silenced its opponents and where student-union officials have been known to unplug the microphones of speakers who transgress their speech codes ('Keep quiet or face arrest' May 11th 2002).

In The Rage against God *you wrote: 'Britain's next monarch is likely to be crowned in a multi-faith ceremony whose main significance will be that it will be the first Coronation not to be explicitly Christian in more than a thousand years. The Rage against God is loose, and is preparing to strip the remaining altars when it is strong enough to do so.' Why do you believe the loss of Christianity is such a tragedy for Britain?*

Did I use the over-used word 'tragedy'? I hope not. It will change Britain into a different place. Our laws, customs, landscape, architecture, town-planning, styles of dress, music, art, literature, education, science, sports, eating and drinking habits, language, sexual conduct and child-rearing have for more than a thousand years been founded on Christianity. Without it, we will be a wholly different country. Maybe people want this. But I doubt very much whether most of them realise the profundity of the changes that will follow once Christianity is finally discarded.

6

Third Timeline 2010–2015

For rulers are not a terror to good works, but to the evil. Wilt thou then not be afraid of the power? do that which is good, and thou shalt have praise of the same (Romans 13:3).

2010 continuing

May: A hung Parliament was the result of the General Election. But after five days of negotiations, the Conservatives, who had won the largest number of seats in the House of Commons (307), formed a coalition government with the Liberal Democrats (57). On Tuesday May 11th Conservative leader David Cameron became Prime Minister; Liberal Democrat leader Nick Clegg became Deputy Prime Minister. They held a joint press conference in the Downing Street rose garden.

The Crown Prosecution Service (CPS) announced on May 17th that it was dropping charges against a Cumbrian street preacher, Dale Mcalpine, whom police had arrested in Workington town centre in April for allegedly breaching the Public Order Act 1986. Mr Mcalpine spent seven hours in a police cell during which he sang Christian hymns and prayed.

Before the CPS decision, *The Daily Mail* on May 1st had

reported on Mr Mcalpine's ordeal: 'Dale Mcalpine was handing out leaflets to shoppers when he told a passer-by and a gay police community support officer that, as a Christian, he believed homosexuality was one of a number of sins that go against the word of God. Mr Mcalpine said that he did not repeat his remarks on homosexuality when he preached from the top of a stepladder after his leafleting. But he has been told that police officers are alleging they heard him making his remarks to a member of the public in a loud voice that could be overheard by others.'

Applauding the CPS's decision to drop the case, homosexual campaigner Peter Tatchell, director of the Peter Tatchell Foundation, wrote on its website (May 17th): 'Although I disagree with Dale McAlpine (*sic*) and support protests against his homophobic views, he should not have been arrested and charged. Criminalisation is a step too far. Despite my opposition to his opinions, I defend his right to freedom of expression. Soon after I offered to appear as a defence witness and to argue in court for Mr McAlpine's acquittal, the Crown Prosecution Service dropped the case.'

July: Gateshead Council admitted it had broken the law when it deregistered an evangelical Christian foster carer for allowing a 16-year-old Muslim girl to choose to be baptised. The council had wanted the girl to stay away from church for six months so that she could take part in what it described as 'normal' teenage activity. Supported by the Christian Institute's Legal Defence Fund, the foster carer brought a Judicial Review against the council's action. The Christian Institute later reported: 'The foster carer's lawyers said the Council had failed to take account of the girl's right to religious liberty and had acted disproportionately in deregistering the foster carer. The Council eventually admitted liability.'[1]

Terry Sanderson, President of the National Secular Society, said: 'The right to change one's religion is guaranteed in just about every human rights charter ever written. It was not the council's place to enforce Islamic rules of apostasy—if that is what they were doing. It is surely a matter of conscience for the individual to decide what religion they want to belong to, if any. At 16, this girl could already have been confirmed into the Catholic or Anglican Church.'[2]

September: Following the resignation of Gordon Brown, former Energy Secretary and MP for Doncaster North, Ed Miliband, was elected leader of the Labour Party, beating his brother, former Foreign Secretary David Miliband, by a small margin. Conservative Party Chairman Baroness Warsi congratulated Mr Miliband on becoming Leader of the Opposition, but she told BBC News he owed his victory to votes of trade unionists, which she feared would lead to an 'abandonment of the centre ground' by Labour.

December: Dale Mcalpine won £7000 in damages after his wrongful arrest. Mr Mcalpine said: 'I forgive the police for how they treated me and I hope that this doesn't happen to anyone else. Despite my experience I still respect the police. I will pray for them because they have a difficult and sometimes dangerous job.'[3] Amazing Grace was one of the hymns Mr Mcalpine had sung in his police cell.

---

1 'Twenty Years of Christian Influence' *The Christian Institute Annual Review* 2011, p17.
2 'Christian foster carer wins case against council who struck her off because Muslim girl in her care changed religion' National Secular Society, 16th July 2010.
3 http://www.christian.org.uk/case/dale-mcalpine/

2011

March: In the House of Commons, the Conservative MP for Gainsborough, Sir Edward Leigh, called for the reform of Section 5 of the Public Order Act 1986, which outlawed the use of 'insulting' words or behaviour. The ConservativeHome website reported Sir Edward arguing: 'Section 5 of the 1986 Act is a classic example of a law that was brought in for a fair reason, to deal with a particular state of affairs long ago, but has been used in practice for something quite different. It was brought in to tackle hooliganism, but it is increasingly used by police to silence peaceful protestors and street preachers.'

Sir Edward cited the case of Christian hotel owners, Ben and Sharon Vogelenzang. In 2009 they were put on trial under Section 5 for having a breakfast-table dispute with a Muslim guest during which they said that Mohammed was a warlord and that Islamic dress oppressed women. Sir Edward welcomed the fact that the judge threw out the case but highlighted the fact that Merseyside Police had seen fit to apply the law 'to theological debates over breakfast.'

May: Sir Edward tabled an amendment to the government's Protection of Freedoms Bill seeking to lower the threshold for prosecution by removing the word 'insulting' from the Public Order Act 1986, but leaving in place the prohibition against 'abusive' and 'threatening' words or behaviour. No vote was allowed on Sir Edward's amendment.[1]

September: The coalition government announced its intention to allow same-sex marriage by 2015. The BBC

---

[1] 'Speak now or forever hold your peace' *The Christian Institute Annual Review 2012*, p7.

reported: 'Ministers are to launch a consultation next spring on how to open up civil marriage to same-sex couples ahead of the next general election ... The leadership of both coalition parties back the move but it is likely to anger some Conservative activists.' The proposal was not in the Conservative manifesto.

October: In a vindication of Sir Edward Leigh's efforts to safeguard freedom of speech, the government announced a consultation over the reform of Section 5 of the Public Order Act 1986.

Prime Minister David Cameron told delegates to the Conservative Party conference in Manchester: 'I once stood before a Conservative conference and said it shouldn't matter whether commitment was between a man and a woman, a woman and a woman, or a man and another man. You applauded me for that. Five years on, we're consulting on legalising gay marriage. And to anyone who has reservations, I say: Yes, it's about equality, but it's also about something else: commitment. Conservatives believe in the ties that bind us; that society is stronger when we make vows to each other and support each other. So I don't support gay marriage despite being a Conservative. I support gay marriage because I'm a Conservative,' *The Guardian* reported.

November: The High Court in London heard a law suit against Bideford Town Council in Devon over its practice of holding Christian prayers at the beginning of its meetings. An atheist ex-councillor with backing from the National Secular Society had brought the case. Bideford Council was supported by the Christian Institute's Legal Defence Fund.

2012

February: The High Court ruled that local councils had no lawful power to hold prayers during official business. Commenting later on the Bideford case the Christian Institute reported: 'Recognising the damaging consequences this would have for religious freedom, the Communities Secretary Eric Pickles MP (Conservative) fast-tracked the commencement of new laws which override the court's ruling. The newly implemented Localism Act restores the right of councils to hold prayers as part of their formal meetings. The Government also wrote to all local councils in England, telling them that this new law restores their power to hold prayers at official meetings if they want to.'[1]

May: In an intriguing alliance to decriminalise the use of 'insulting' words in public, the Christian Institute joined forces with the National Secular Society and the Peter Tatchell Foundation to launch the Reform Section 5 campaign.

September: Assisted by the Christian Institute's Legal Defence Fund, Lillian Ladele brought her case for 'reasonable accommodation' of her Christian beliefs over the registration of civil partnerships to the European Court of Human Rights (ECHR) in Strasbourg. The British government contested the case.

2013

January: Lillian Ladele finally lost her long-running legal battle when the ECHR dismissed her claim that she had been discriminated against in the workplace and

---

[1]   Ibid. p6

ruled in favour of the British government. Her case was heard along with three other Christians who claimed workplace discrimination.

Writing on *The Guardian's* 'Comment is Free Belief' platform, Mark Hill QC, argued that Miss Ladele was 'the real loser in the four conjoined applications.' He quoted the 'powerful' minority opinion of the two dissenting ECHR judges in the ruling: 'If anything, both the law (the Civil Partnership Act 2004) and the practice of other local authorities allowed for the possibility of compromises which would not force registrars to act against their consciences. In Ladele's case, however, a combination of backstabbing by her colleagues and the blinkered political correctness of the borough of Islington (which clearly favoured "gay rights" over fundamental human rights) eventually led to her dismissal.'

The intriguing alliance between the Christian Institute, the National Secular Society, the Peter Tatchell Foundation, and comedian Rowan Atkinson paid off. After its consultation, the government agreed to the reform of Section 5 of the Public Order Act 1986 and the revised law was supported by Parliament. In its 2013 Annual Review, 'From this day forward' (p6), the Christian Institute reported: 'The new law will come into force when the Home Office issues new guidance for the police. This is good news for free speech.'

February: The coalition government's Marriage (Same Sex Couples) Bill cruised through its second reading in the House of Commons by a majority of 225 MPs. But 139 Conservative MPs opposed the Bill, nearly half of the Parliamentary party. Thirty-five Tories did not vote, so more Conservatives MPs actually voted against the Bill than voted for it. The Bill included the so-called 'quadruple lock' for the

Church of England and the Church in Wales. This prevented these Established Churches from being forced to conduct same-sex marriages by making it illegal for them to do so unless their governing bodies voluntarily chose to opt in.

April: Trinity College Oxford apologised for hosting Christian Concern's Wilberforce Academy conference over the Easter vacation 'in a continuing row over the college's affiliations with a group with allegedly homophobic campaigns,' the *Oxford Student* reported. The paper said: 'In a statement on the college's website, Trinity's President Sir Ivor Roberts said that the college "regrets that any current or old members were upset by the fact that we gave houseroom unwittingly to Christian Concern", promising to allocate any profit from the conference to an appropriate charity.' Christian Concern denied hating homosexual people. In March, when the controversy blew up because of Christian Concern's stand for the traditional definition of marriage, its chief executive, Andrea Minichiello Williams, was quoted in *The Independent* as saying: 'We have immense love for every human being. It is wrong to portray us as an organisation that is motivated by any hatred.'

July: The Marriage (Same Sex Couples) Bill received the Royal Assent, paving the way for legal same-sex marriages in England and Wales in the summer of 2014. The BBC reported Equalities Minister Maria Miller saying that the passing of the bill was 'clear affirmation' that 'respect for each and every person is paramount, regardless of age, religion, gender, ethnicity or sexuality.' But Conservative MP Sir Gerald Howarth, one of the bill's opponents, said it was 'astonishing that a bill for which there is absolutely no mandate, against which a majority of Conservatives voted, has been bulldozed through both Houses.'

November: The Supreme Court ruled against an elderly Christian couple who had been sued for refusing to grant a double-room to a homosexual couple at their Cornish bed and breakfast business. The BBC reported: 'Hazelmary and Peter Bull refused to let civil partners Steven Preddy and Martyn Hall stay in a double room at Chymorvah House in Marazion in Cornwall in 2008. The couple, who had already lost cases at Bristol County Court and the Court of Appeal, said they were "saddened". Mr and Mrs Bull have said they regard any sex outside marriage as a "sin". The Bulls denied discriminating against Mr Hall and Mr Preddy, who are from Bristol. Sixty-nine-year-old Mrs Bull and her 74-year-old husband said their decision was founded on a "religiously-informed judgment of conscience". Five Supreme Court justices ruled against them on Wednesday after analysing the case at a hearing in London in October.'

2014

February: The removal of 'insulting' words from the scope of Section 5 of the Public Order Act 1986 came into force.

March: After what the Christian Institute described as 'one of the worst cases of infringement of the religious liberty' it had ever seen, Christian street preacher John Craven received £13,000 in compensation after being wrongfully arrested for quoting from the Bible in public. As the Christian Institute later described Mr Craven's ordeal: 'Police in Manchester held Mr Craven in custody for over 19 hours, following a complaint from two teenagers. When the youths had asked him what he thought of homosexuality, he responded by explaining what the Bible says. For nearly 15 hours in custody Mr Craven was denied food and access to medication for his rheumatoid arthritis. Days before the case was due to go to court, the police settled the claim for wrongful arrest, false imprisonment and breach of his human rights. The total cost for Greater Manchester Police, including both parties' legal bills, came to over £50,000.'[1]

July: The Northern Ireland Equality Commission confirmed that it was supporting a potential legal action for discrimination against a bakery firm run by Christians in Northern Ireland. Ashers Baking Company declined an order from a homosexual activist with the Queer Space group. He had ordered a cake featuring the Sesame Street puppets, Bert and Ernie, and bearing the slogan 'Support Gay Marriage.' The BBC reported: 'The County Antrim firm could face legal action from the Equality Commission. The watchdog confirmed it is assisting the customer whose order was refused and has written to the baking company on his behalf. The cake was ordered for a civic event in Bangor Castle Town Hall, County Down, to mark International Day Against Homophobia and Transphobia.'

Ashers' 24-year-old general manager, Daniel McArthur, said marriage in Northern Ireland 'still is defined as being a union between one man and one woman' and said his company was taking 'a stand.' The firm was being supported by the Christian Institute.

September: Ahead of the Conservative Party conference in October, Home Secretary Theresa May revealed that 'the Conservative manifesto will contain pledges to introduce banning orders for extremist groups and extremism disruption orders for extremists who spread hate but do not break existing laws,' according to a briefing note distributed

---

1   'Do not hinder them' *The Christian Institute Annual Review 2015*, p7

to journalists. *The Guardian* reported: 'The orders would be issued by a high court judge on an application from the police on the lower legal test of "balance of probabilities" rather than the stronger test of "beyond reasonable doubt."'

October: Dominic Raab, Conservative MP for Esher and Walton, raised concerns about the implications of the Home Secretary's extremism disruption plans for Christian freedom of expression. Writing in *The Daily Telegraph*, he argued: 'The public should certainly expect the security services to track terrorists online, but the broad powers of proposed Extremism Disruption Orders (EDO) could be abused. Those engaged in passionate debates—such as Christians objecting to gay marriage—could find themselves slapped down.'

2015

March: In what became known as the 'gay cake' case, homosexual activist Gareth Lee, backed financially by the NI Equality Commission, brought his suit for discrimination against Ashers Bakery before district judge Isobel Brownlie in Belfast County Court. Judge Brownlie reserved judgement after the three-day hearing, *The Belfast Telegraph* reported.

Prime Minister David Cameron fired the starting gun for the May 7th General Election by informing the Queen of the dissolution of Parliament. The General Election date—the first Thursday in May after every five years—was set by the Fixed Term Parliament Act 2011.

April: The Conservatives' election manifesto promised a referendum on Britain's membership of the European Union by 2017.

7
Fourth Timeline 2015–2017

Pilate therefore said unto him, Art thou a king then? Jesus answered, Thou sayest that I am a king. To this end was I born, and for this cause came I into the world, that I should bear witness unto the truth. Every one that is of the truth heareth my voice. Pilate saith unto him, What is truth? (John 18:37–38a).

2015 continued

May: The Conservatives won the General Election with 331 seats in the House of Commons, a gain of 24 giving them a working majority of 12 MPs. The Liberal Democrats suffered an electoral meltdown losing 49 seats leaving them with 8 MPs. The Scottish National Party gained 50 seats, most of them from Labour, giving them 56 MPs in Westminster.

In the 'gay cake' case in Belfast, Judge Brownlie ruled against Ashers Bakery in favour of Gareth Lee. The BBC reported: 'Damages of £500 were agreed in advance by legal teams on both sides of the dispute. A lawyer for Mr Lee said the money would be donated to charity.' The BBC's religious affairs correspondent, Caroline Wyatt, commented: 'This case has highlighted once again the continuing tensions in the UK between equality law and freedom of conscience for those whose religious beliefs don't allow them to accept same-sex marriage.'

Backed by the Christian Institute, Ashers said they would appeal the ruling.

September: Following the resignation of Ed Miliband, Jeremy Corbyn, MP for Islington North, was elected leader of the Labour Party with a large mandate from its membership. A socialist by conviction and a consistent opponent of the Iraq war, Mr Corbyn faced a fraught relationship with Blairite MPs in the Parliamentary Labour Party.

2016

January: The chief inspector of Britain's state schools, the head of Ofsted Sir Michael Wilshaw, told LBC radio that as part of its counter-extremism strategy 'the government wants Sunday schools, and wants Madrassas and after-school clubs to be registered. We will not be inspecting every one of them—but we will know that they exist.' He later backtracked on these comments under questioning from a Conservative MP in a Parliamentary session on Multi-Academy trusts.[1]

February: Prime Minister David Cameron announced that the Referendum on Britain's membership of the EU would be held on June 23rd.

March: A Christian family court magistrate in Kent was

---

1   Christian Concern, Ofsted chief backtracks on Sunday school regulation comments, June 17th 2016.

sacked after saying in a BBC television interview in March 2015: 'My responsibility as a magistrate, as I saw it, was to do what I considered best for the child, and my feeling was therefore that it would be better if it was a man and woman who were the adopted parents.' Richard Page, 68, was speaking to the BBC after he had been disciplined in 2014 for arguing privately to colleagues during an adoption case against a child being adopted by a homosexual couple and saying that the child would be better placed with a mother and father. Mr Page had served fifteen years as a magistrate in Maidstone and Sevenoaks. The Christian Legal Centre was acting for Mr Page.

Andrea Minichiello Williams said: 'The Lord Chancellor has removed Richard from the magistracy for allegedly being "prejudiced" and for speaking out in the media about what has happened to him. This unmasks the face of the new political orthodoxy; it is unkind. It tries to silence opposing views and if it fails it crushes and punishes the person who holds those views. To remove someone like Richard from the bench is modern day madness. He has a lifetime of public service, expertise in mental health. He is motivated by his Christian faith and a deep compassion for people,' *The Daily Mail* reported.

May: The 'gay cake' case appeal by Ashers Bakery went before the Royal Courts of Justice in Belfast. The judges reserved judgement.

June: A majority of Britons who participated in the Referendum—52 per cent amounting to 17 million people—voted to leave the European Union. On the morning after the vote, David Cameron announced his intention to step down as Prime Minister. In front of Number 10 Downing Street he declared: 'I think the country requires fresh leadership to take it in this direction. I will do everything I can as Prime Minister to steady the ship over the coming weeks and months but I do not think it would be right for me to try to be the captain that steers our country to its next destination,' *The Daily Telegraph* reported.

July: The Iraq Inquiry, begun in 2009 and chaired by Sir John Chilcot, finally published its report. The Chilcot report found that the 2003 invasion was not the 'last resort' action presented to MPs and the public. It found that there was no 'imminent threat' from Saddam and the intelligence case was 'not justified,' the BBC reported, adding that Mr Blair apologised for any mistakes made but not for the decision to go to war.

After her main rival Andrea Leadsom, MP for South Northamptonshire, withdrew from the contest, Theresa May was elected leader of the Conservative Party and thus Britain's second woman Prime Minister. In his farewell speech in front of Downing Street, Mr Cameron cited the introduction of same-sex marriage as one of the main achievements of his premiership.

The former head of MI5, Sir Jonathan Evans, warned that the government's proposed counter-extremism measures could lead to crackdowns on 'harmless evangelical street preachers.' Writing in *The Daily Telegraph* Sir Jonathan cautioned that 'definitions will be crucial' in the upcoming extremism Bill, and noted that its implementation 'will be fraught with risk.' Sir Jonathan, who served as Director General of the security intelligence agency between 2007 and 2013, said he could imagine Christian preachers being targeted 'out of misplaced zeal.'[1]

October: Ashers Bakery lost its appeal. The *Daily Mail* reported: 'In delivering the appeal judgment, Northern Ireland's Lord Chief Justice Sir Declan Morgan said Ashers had directly discriminated. He rejected the argument that the bakery would be endorsing the slogan by baking the cake. "The fact that a baker provides a cake for a particular team or portrays witches on a Halloween cake does not indicate any support for either," he said. In a 30-minute ruling, Sir Declan said the original judgment had been correct in finding that 'as a matter of law Ashers had discriminated against the respondent directly on the grounds of sexual orientation.'

Quoted in the paper, Peter Tatchell said: 'The judgment opens a can of worms. It means that a Muslim printer could be obliged to publish cartoons of Mohammed and a Jewish printer could be required to publish a book that propagates Holocaust denial. It could also encourage far-right extremists to demand that bakers and other service providers facilitate the promotion of anti-immigrant and anti-Muslim opinions. What the court has decided sets a dangerous, authoritarian precedent that is open to serious abuse. Discrimination against people should be illegal but not discrimination against ideas and opinions.'

December: Ashers Bakery confirmed that it would take its appeal to the Supreme Court. The Court later agreed to hear the case in October 2017. The Christian Institute continued to support Ashers out of its Legal Defence Fund.

---

[1] 'Ex-spy chief: "Anti-extremist" law could target preachers' The Christian Institute, 2nd July 2015.

2017

January: The government's top social integration adviser, Dame Louise Casey, told a parliamentary hearing that it was unacceptable for Roman Catholic schools to oppose same-sex marriage. 'It is not OK for Catholic schools to be homophobic and anti gay marriage. That is not OK either— it is not how we bring children up in this country,' *The Catholic Herald* reported. She continued: 'It is often veiled as religious conservatism, and I have a problem with the expression "religious conservatism", because often it can be anti-equalities.'

April: Theresa May called for a General Election on June 8th. Because of the Fixed Term Parliament Act she required a two thirds majority in the House of Commons for an election three years early, which she obtained.

The High Court granted a Christian social work student permission to mount a judicial review after he had been removed from his two-year MA course at Sheffield University for expressing his beliefs. Felix Ngole, 39, had said during a Facebook debate in 2016 that 'the Bible and God identify homosexuality as a sin.' *The Daily Telegraph* reported: 'He is thought to be the first claimant to challenge a decision which barred him from a profession because his religious beliefs made him "unfit to practice".' Mr Ngole was being backed by the Christian Legal Centre.

Writing in *The Sun*, columnist Rod Liddle declared: 'Frankly, I think our social services departments could do with rather more people who have strong, Christian principles instead of the inept, hand-wringing, liberal halfwits who allowed the vile sexual abuse of children to go on across the country ... But even that's not the main point.

Universities are supposed to be places where a huge diversity of views can be heard. Not any more, not in our universities. If you don't subscribe to every one of their modern, secular, liberal beliefs you're out on your ear. Either banned from speaking at their campuses or thrown off your course. Just because you believe in something that they don't.'

May: An Islamist terrorist murdered 22 people and injured 120 at a pop concert at the Manchester Arena. Islamic State used the Telegram electronic messaging app to claim responsibility for the attack: 'One of the soldiers of the Caliphate was able to place an explosive device within a gathering of the Crusaders in the city of Manchester.'

Liberal Democrat leader Tim Farron, MP for Westmorland and Lonsdale, who was known to belong to an evangelical Christian church, faced repeated questions by the media about whether he believed gay sex was a sin. He eventually said he did not believe it was. In an interview with the BBC's political correspondent Eleanor Garnier, he said he had not wanted 'to get into a series of questions unpicking the theology of the Bible,' but told her: 'I don't believe that gay sex is a sin.'

June: A hung Parliament was the result of the General Election. The Conservatives lost 13 seats wiping out their House of Commons majority and leaving them with 318 MPs. The Labour Party under Jeremy Corbyn, who been re-elected leader in 2016 after attempts by Blairite Labour MPs to remove him, gained 30 seats giving it 262 MPs. The Liberal Democrats were up by 4 to 12 seats. The Scottish Nationalists reduced to 35.

Mrs May began negotiations with Northern Ireland's Democratic Unionist Party, which had 10 MPs, over forming a coalition government, and on that basis Her Majesty the Queen offered her an opportunity to form a government. The DUP's support for traditional marriage came in for severe criticism in the mainstream media. Writing in *The Daily Mail*, former *Daily Mirror* editor and *Good Morning Britain* TV presenter Piers Morgan accused Mrs May of 'actively plotting a desperate, dirty coalition government with the dinosaur DUP bigots in Northern Ireland to save your own skin.'

Tim Farron resigned as leader of the Liberal Democrats stating that he had found it impossible to reconcile his Christian faith with the demands of leading a 'progressive' political party. In his resignation speech he said: 'At the start of this election, I found myself under scrutiny again—asked about matters to do with my faith. I felt guilty that this focus was distracting attention from our campaign, obscuring our message. Journalists have every right to ask what they see fit. The consequences of the focus on my faith is that I have found myself torn between living as a faithful Christian and serving as a political leader. A better, wiser person than me may have been able to deal with this more successfully, to have remained faithful to Christ while leading a political party in the current environment. To be a political leader— especially of a progressive, liberal party in 2017—and to live as a committed Christian, to hold faithfully to the Bible's teaching, has felt impossible for me,' *The Guardian* reported.

But the last word on the timelines goes to the valiant Christian Institute. On the day after the General Election, its deputy director Simon Calvert urged supporters to pray for those in authority: 'The Government and Parliament have a difficult job ahead. There is no doubt that Islamist terrorism poses a very serious threat. We strongly support efforts to combat terrorism and the ideologies which underpin it, but it is vital that the political response is focussed on the cause of these attacks—Islamism—and that Christian freedoms and the civil liberties of innocent citizens are not jeopardised."[1]

1 'Pray for those in authority' The Christian Institute, 9th June 2017

8

Britain AD 2050—Islam Dominant

And they worshipped the dragon which gave power unto the beast: and they worshipped the beast, saying, Who is like unto the beast? who is able to make war with him? (Revelation 13:4).

My name is Fatima, but I was baptised as Grace. I was born into a British Christian family of West Indian origin in south London in 2015.

I am writing this using old-fashioned pen and paper. Electronic devices are closely monitored by the authorities so it would be too dangerous to write this in the normal way. I intend to put this testimony in my pocket-sized paper Christian Bible which I have concealed in the women's toilet in our local mosque and which I read whenever I can.

Britain became a Muslim country in 2040. In 2030 the banking system of what was then the United Kingdom collapsed and the government no longer had the financial resources to shore up the high street banks. Unlike in the 2008 crash when the UK government was able to inject money into the banks, this time around there really were angry queues at the cash points with people unable to get their money out.

Because of its overwhelming debt the British government could no longer borrow on the international money markets. They initially turned to the United States of America for a national emergency loan but this was refused because of entrenched anti-British sentiment in that country. So the British government appealed to Saudi Arabia.

The Saudi government baled the British economy out but the political price was increased influence for Wahhabi Islam at every level of British society. There was already a strong Muslim foundation to build on.

Due to its healthy birth-rate compared to the secular British, the Muslim proportion of the population had been growing rapidly in the first quarter of the twenty-first century and by 2030 had reached twenty per cent. It was hitting about five per cent in England when I was a baby.[1] The increasing incapacity of the National Health Service in the 2020s reduced the elderly British population, so that boosted the younger Muslim proportion. The Muslim population was also boosted by a flow of secular-background British people converting to Islam in that decade. They turned to Islam after becoming disillusioned with the permissive society rotting as it was in economic failure.

In 2035, whilst I was studying Philosophy, Politics and Economics at Oxford University, women lost the vote. By then male suffrage had already been significantly reduced with voting rights restricted to practising Muslims of five years' standing. It has to be said that the secular British middle classes, numbed by political correctness and economic

---

1   http://www.telegraph.co.uk/news/12132641/Number-of-UK-Muslims-exceeds-three-million-for-first-time.html

stagnation, were pretty docile in the face of such loss of democratic privileges hard won by their ancestors.

But the pathway to a Wahhabi Islamic state became clear in 2036 when violent social disorder erupted in major British cities. To quote the twentieth-century rock band, Pink Floyd, which my older brother used to listen to, 'the rusty wire that holds the cork that keeps the anger in'[1] gave way in a deeply divided society and a tsunami of human evil devastated Britain's cities.

The British government did not have the necessary resources to restore order to the streets and so appealed to the Saudis for military assistance. Saudi troops were airlifted in and Britain was put under martial law.

When it came under a Saudi-style absolute monarchy in 2040, Britain was renamed the United Kingdom of Islam (UKI). Northern Ireland had already merged with the Republic of Ireland in 2030, so technically I suppose the United Kingdom had already ended as an entity but the new Muslim government clearly liked the ring of the name.

United Ireland still allows churches to operate under strict licensing but it is likely that its government will soon close these down for the sake of closer relations with the now economically thriving UKI.

The British king was forced to abdicate in 2040. Because of his contacts with the Saudi royal family he, his wife and children were allowed to leave the country and the Polish government granted them asylum. No members of the extended former royal family were allowed to leave.

---

1   From 'Two Suns in the Sunset,' *The Final Cut*, 1983.

The Free Britain movement, which is not exclusively Christian in its membership but is largely led by committed Christian exiles, is based in Warsaw. It does its best to communicate Christian material through its websites and its satellite broadcasting arm to the UKI. But the government has become increasingly adept at tracking these communications and individuals found to have accessed Christian material from Warsaw have been arrested.

There are no churches in the UKI. I attend the mosque but I pray to God the Father through Jesus Christ our Lord, as I was taught as a child and as I decided to do myself when I chose to be baptised as a teenager in the lively church I loved to belong to in London.

In 2041 I became the third wife of a polygamous Muslim man. I have three children and my eldest son is now eight years old.

I have not told my children that I am a Christian but my son is beginning to ask me questions about my parents and my childhood. I believe that the time is coming when I should tell him the truth about what I am—for the sake of his own soul in fact. I do not believe that I should withhold the gospel of God's saving love in the Lord Jesus from him and from my younger children when they are older.

I would have to warn them of the consequences for me of apostasy under Sharia law if they told my husband or indeed anyone else. But I am becoming convinced that I should take the risk. That is why I am putting this testimony in writing and placing it in my Bible.

I am signing this with my real Christian name—Grace.

9
Britain AD 2050—Religion Banned (Part One)

The fool hath said in his heart, There is no God. They are corrupt, they have done abominable works, there is none that doeth good (Psalm 14:1).

Here, imagining himself as a leader in the underground British Christian movement in 2050, Andrew Symes gives an interview to the fictional Free Christian Britain website based in Warsaw, Poland.

How did public religion come to be banned in Britain?

It came about because of the three-way battle in the West between secular humanism, militant Islam and orthodox Christianity, and the eventual victory for a repressive form of secularism.

If we go further back in history, the 1960s saw the beginnings of a wholesale retreat of orthodox Christianity away from the public space (government, media, the arts, education) to focus on church-based evangelism and mission. This was done for good reasons: an awareness of large numbers of nominal Christians in the pews, and a growing proportion of the nation's population who were completely unreached by the gospel.

Vibrant evangelical Christianity unconsciously developed a culture whereby the really keen disciples were expected to be overseas missionaries or full-time Christian workers in Britain. Taking seriously Jesus' warning about love of power and status meant that committed and gifted lay people became more involved in church and less likely to seek promotion in the professions, and so become key influencers of policy. While a few individual Christians tried to make headway in the arts and media, they were often unsupported by churches, and were too small a minority to make a difference in the field.

Various forms of secularism rose up to fill the void: a belief in science and the law as being the ultimate authority, a libertarian and sometimes neo-pagan rejoicing in throwing off the shackles of what was seen as outdated superstition and oppressive morality, and a more aggressive openly anti-Christian humanism. Liberal Christianity, previously confined to the ivory towers of academia and the cloisters of Cathedral closes, moved out into a friendly engagement and alliance with these new forms of liberalism in secular culture.

The place of sexual politics, and the failure of the church to meet the challenge of secularism's radical redefinition of marriage, family and traditional understandings of what it means to be human, should not be underestimated. In the 1960s and 1970s, gay rights activists in the West were seen as underground and revolutionary, often in alliance with radical feminists and Marxists in wanting to overturn what they saw as a bourgeois system of unfair capitalism and oppressive morality.

A massive change occurred in the 1980s, with the advent of AIDS and the collapse of Russian communism. Gays and 'commies' had a bad name and the image needed to change. So a campaign began on several fronts—education, the law, media—to make the ideas and vision of the Left attractive again. The strategy of the 'cultural Marxists' and the new LGBT activists was to move sexual 'liberation' and the narrative of 'oppressor' (white, straight, cisgender, wealthy, male) and 'victim' (non-white, LGBT, poor, female) away from the revolutionary fringe into the mainstream of culture. No longer against the establishment and counter-cultural, but controlling the establishment and accepted as normal in the culture.

The way to this would be by the constant repetition of memes and narratives, for example the existence of 'gay' and 'trans' as an innate, unchangeable category of person, on a par with biological gender and race; the universal and unfair oppression of such people, and the urgent need for complete removal of 'discrimination' and any bar to 'full inclusion.' These ideas would be reinforced by respectable bodies, though with no basis in science or theology. They would always be prefaced by such phrases as 'everyone knows that ...' and 'all sensible people believe that ...'

Those from the establishment who changed their mind and supported the new ideas would be feted as progressive and caring; those who opposed would be demonised as bigoted, old-fashioned, and linked to Nazism. At the same time there would be wholesale denial of any philosophy behind this campaign: we would hear constantly that 'there is no "gay agenda" there are just gay people to have sympathy for.'

Emblematic symbols would eventually complete the first

stage of the revolution: the redefinition of marriage to include couples of the same sex, the redefinition of gender to mean how a person felt rather than what they are physically, and the transformation of Gay Pride (previously an aggressive, obscene and revolutionary protest) into family-friendly festivals sponsored by the biggest capitalist corporates. These major societal changes only required careful influencing and intimidation of a small number of lawmakers and business chiefs rather than the whole population.

As with all revolutions, the sexual revolution was content to persuade by pushing a 'positive' message about pansexual freedom through media and education. It also sought to silence opposition by creating simple memes such as 'homophobia' i.e. bringing the focus on the so-called oppression of people rather than the underlying ideas behind 'gay' and 'trans,' and then by use of the law.

In the end, the suppression of orthodox Christianity and the promotion of LGBT ideology came down to the coming together of the thinking of previously distinct and even opposing groups now dominating the British establishment in the new Millennium—politicians and civil servants concerned most of all with civil order and the restraint of conflict; libertarian sexual revolutionaries who believe that all taboos around sex should be removed for the sake of human flourishing; radical socialists who see sexual and monetary restraint as part of oppressive bourgeois values; atheist humanists who believe that religion causes conflict and religion-based ethics prevent progress; and radical capitalists who see opportunities for marketing and financial gain in the increased sexualisation of society, especially the youth (in fields of medicine, law, fashion etc., but also in pornography and sex trafficking).

In 2022 a Labour government was elected after a period when the Conservatives, already weakened and then having failed to deliver a clean exit from the European Union, limped to an inevitable defeat. Labour embarked on fulfilling its manifesto of huge public borrowing and spending, and eradicating what it saw as the last vestiges of social conservatism.

Over the next ten years church and other religious schools were abolished, and control over all curricula for Religious Education was given to a 'neutral' body consisting of eminent atheists and secular humanists. This affected schools, universities and theological colleges in terms of the content of what was permissible to be taught and studied. The House of Lords was reformed with the number of bishops reduced to ten, then to just the Archbishops of Canterbury and York, alongside individual representatives from other religions.

Pressure continued to build on permitting the deliberate ending of life for the elderly and infirm. Parliament voted to allow a form of euthanasia in 2025, and shortly after this, the availability of a new drug which gave the user extremely pleasant sensations and hallucinations before sleep and death led to a steep rise in the take-up of the service, available freely on the NHS. In 2035 there were 250,000 abortions and 70,000 terminations of life for mostly elderly adults.

At the same time, incidents of Islamic terrorism increased. There were bans on extremist imams, but many commentators and politicians were uncomfortable about this, saying repeatedly in public that the problem was 'extremist religious doctrine,' not Islam. Again and again acts of jihadist terror were compared to assassinations of abortion doctors by Christian extremists (of which there were two recorded instances in the US, back in the early 2000s), small demonstrations by right-wing groups such as the English Defence League, and mental health problems suffered by gay people, attributed to Christian teaching. Jesus' teaching on hell was routinely quoted on TV and radio discussion shows, and social media, as illustrations of Christian extremism which had no place in modern Britain, along with violent passages in the Qu'ran.

The result was the Extremism Suppression Bill of 2032, which prohibited any public expression of any views deemed to be offensive, abusive or harmful, and specifically included biblical Christian teaching on hell, the uniqueness of Christ, and sexual ethics.

In the same year the Church of England General Synod, now with only a handful of conservatives, passed a motion to similar effect, and in fact in 2030 Church House also published a new Authorised Version Bible which had removed any potentially offensive or extremist material. After this, repression of religious freedom became more commonplace: parents with socially conservative views based on religion were frequently questioned and cautioned by police. Youth groups and church websites were monitored, street preaching was prohibited and some Christian mission organisations closed down.

Why was there such overwhelming public support for a ban on religion rather than allowing churches and mosques etc. to register?

Initially in 2032 all religious organisations had to register with the government, and fill in lengthy forms detailing their beliefs. Most churches complied. Some found ways of dissembling on the forms, concealing orthodox Christian belief in vague jargon while continuing to worship and teach as before; others refused to comply, and began to operate as unlicensed or underground churches. Police forces established anti-extremism compliance officers who had powers to attend church and mosque meetings in plain clothes to monitor what was being taught. A number of pastors were fined and in some cases, jailed, as were lay people who crossed boundaries in sharing their faith. Britain was a predominantly Protestant country which only seventeen years previously had seen many evangelical churches and networks celebrate 500 years since the Reformation. But ironically in 2034 more Roman Catholic and black Pentecostal clergy were punished by the State for illegal religious gatherings or for 'extremist' language, than evangelical Protestants.

White middle class evangelicals and other Christians prepared to speak up publicly against the restrictions on religious freedom were very few and easily isolated and picked off by the end of the 2020s. However, one group of Christians refused to accept what was happening and became increasingly militant in the 2030s.

Large scale immigration had seen the establishment of enormous congregations of Pentecostal Christians, mostly in London and from African heritage. The first generation of leaders had been very keen to build bridges with politicians and be accepted and respected as important community leaders. There was a split in the second generation, however, with the establishment of the militant Christian sect, the Jesus Resistance Army. They began by forming self-defence units to protect Christian families and small churches against increasingly violent attacks by criminal gangs and Muslim activists.

Their leaders initially sought to involve the police, but then made a series of public statements accompanying horrific video footage posted on media outlets, showing the police standing by while churches were burned, or doing nothing in response to testimony from Christian women about harassment and rape. In some of the major cities of Britain, they said, Christians were being driven out of neighbourhoods which were becoming either lawless or exclusively Muslim. The government was doing nothing for fear of being branded as Islamophobic, and because their mantra remained that all problems in society were as a result of inequality between rich and poor, and the legacy of Tory rule.

Two weeks of violent unrest erupted in August 2037 in parts of east and north London between jihadist gangs and mostly African-origin members of the Jesus Resistance Army. Though some courageous local reporters tried to show that the Christian elements were operating in self-defence, the overwhelming narrative in the secular press and in Parliament was 'this is the fault of religion.'

The 'Battle of Hackney' shocked the nation and turned the spotlight on the government as well as organised religion. The economy was in recession after years of poor financial management and a mountain of debt that was similar to Greece twenty years previously. The country of England (Scotland, Wales and Ireland now formed the new Federation of Celtic Republics) was increasingly divided along race, class and economic lines, intra-religious conflict in the inner cities was now out of control, and the clamour for change in the form of strong and authoritative government became irresistible.

A new party, the National Progressive Alliance, had been formed in 2030. It was strongly secular, with a radically individualist view of humanity. It was strongly 'right wing' in its economic policies, its advocacy of radical cuts to benefits for those who don't or can't work, its restrictions on immigration and foreign aid. But it was radically progressive in wanting to increase the power of the State in a number of areas, not just promoting liberal views of the family, sex, gender, euthanasia etc, but in advocating suppression of religion and in fact all socially conservative ideologies.

The majority of the population felt that radical Islam in particular had been permitted to flourish. The Labour government had focussed their repression on Christianity which required simply the passing of laws—Christians could generally be expected to obey them—and through attacks on social media, intimidating, ridiculing, and damaging reputations. Islamists were not easy to control by these methods, and there was increasing clamour for a much tougher approach, including armed police and an end to areas of cities dominated by Muslim gangs.

The NPA came to power in 2037. In 2040 they implemented a complete ban on all public expression of religion. All churches, mosques, synagogues and temples were closed. Gatherings of up to twelve people for religious purposes were permitted in private homes or non-religious buildings, but required a licence which could take up to six months to obtain. No advertising of religious meetings was allowed. There was a complete ban on proselytisation, on publishing and distributing religious literature or media of any kind. No-one known to adhere to a religion was eligible for public office such as local government, the law or teaching. Families known to have links to religion were assigned a state advisor who would regularly monitor what was being passed on to children.

In some areas with large Muslim populations there were demonstrations and attempts to enter mosques. The response of the government was swift and unequivocal, with the police and army on the streets in large numbers.

After a relatively short time, the situation was largely accepted. A substantial number of Muslims and a few Christians emigrated over the next ten years.

10

Britain AD 2050—Religion
Banned (Part Two)

*But Peter and John answered and said unto them, Whether
it be right in the sight of God to hearken unto you more than
unto God, judge ye. For we cannot but speak the things we
have seen and heard* (Acts 4:19–20).

The imaginary scenario continues.

*What broadly was the spiritual condition of
the mainline British Churches by the time
their public worship came to be banned?*

Methodists and United Reformed churches had already
ceased to exist by the time the ban came in. Churches in
the Baptist Union and the Church of England were almost
entirely liberal and positive towards the changes in society,
apart from some charismatic evangelicals who retained some
aspects of historic biblical teaching but focussed largely on a
pietistic spirituality and local pastoral ministry, and did not
address controversial issues at all. There was no tradition of
protest or prophetic confrontation with the culture in these
churches, and so they accepted the closure, advising their

members to be open to the Spirit in everyday life for their own personal enrichment, and to pray and do good for others.

Those who suffered most from the new laws were Roman Catholics and ritual-centred Anglicans, whose spirituality was more tied to church buildings than evangelical Protestants who morphed more easily into house fellowships. While many churches had closed through declining number over the previous twenty years, there were still substantial numbers of buildings where worship took place every week. Many of them still boasted historic architecture and good music, underpinned by forms of prayer and, in some cases, the teaching of biblical faith. Over its church closure policy, the English government was put under more pressure from overseas bodies such as the United Nations, influenced by the Vatican, than it was by any protest movement at home, although English Roman Catholics did offer some protest.

The general condition of mainline churches overall in the decade leading up to the ban could be said to be theologically strongly influenced by liberal philosophy and theology. In denial about what was happening in the culture, the churches which retained some connection with orthodox belief were inward looking, tolerant of doctrinal error and sin, not wanting to jeopardise material comfort.

It was common for their leaders to blame those who warned about the coming restrictions on freedom, and in fact most of those who determined to follow biblical faith left the mainline churches in the 2020s and 2030s for independent fellowships.

What social difference has the ban on public religion made?

The government found itself having to become increasingly

repressive in enforcing a value system deliberately shorn of religious foundations. Detailed laws were formulated for more and more behaviours which previously had been left to the discretion and common sense of individuals.

Schools 25 years previously reported that many of the new generation of students, with no Christian background at home, at school or in the media, were openly questioning ideas which had previously been axiomatic, for example 'why should we help the poor?' Society became increasingly nastier, and people more selfish.

The link between the often chaotic lifestyles and high prevalence of crime and educational underachievement in areas of low churchgoing such as council estates had often been noted. Similar issues: instability of relationships, low levels of marriage, youth delinquency, mental illness and drug use were now increasingly common in more affluent areas.

Although all public manifestation of religion was banned (including for example, new age-type gatherings), there was a resurgence of interest in private esoteric spiritualities, tarot reading, séances, fortune telling etc. Large public assemblies such as sports events at times took on a semi-religious flavour. The 'cult' of celebrity, and the constant focus in the media on encouraging people to 'be their true selves' encouraged a worldview in which technology was to be the servant of the narcissistic individual who is god in his own universe, rather than the Christian idea of worshipping God and serving others.

What is life like for you as a leader in the underground Christian movement in this society?

The government is now using increasingly sophisticated

technology to intercept electronic communication, so the small fellowships which continued to meet unofficially and secretly have to operate by word of mouth, and even old fashioned paper mail which was ironically more secure than e-messaging. In some ways it has been like a return to the days of the early church, when books and electronically distributed articles are subject to censorship, so the emphasis has to be on face to face teaching, worship and discipleship in small groups and one to one.

The underground church also has to be much more local in its focus. While it is still possible to obtain news of national and worldwide Christian events and thinking, this usually has to be done in the form of distribution, by hand, of home-produced materials, and verbal updates in small groups.

The fellowship and pastoral care is much more intense and genuine that it often was in the past. People literally put their lives in the hands of God and of their fellow Christians. There is very little superficiality. Christians are serious about their faith. All night prayer meetings occur regularly. People share their possessions with one another. At the small fellowships, which don't only occur on Sunday but can be held at irregular times during the week to avoid the attentions of the religion police, sermons of an hour will often be followed by intense discussion of the Bible and how it can be put into practice, sometimes for two hours after the 'service' has ended.

People meet in homes, usually after dark. If they come by car they park a couple of streets away and arrive at different times. Singing during worship is not usually possible, but sometimes sung worship can occur in meetings which take place in woods.

For leaders, there is on the one hand intense pressure. There is the constant fear of being arrested. Spouses, usually wives of underground church pastors, have to be fully supportive of the role, and give up any of the normal expectations of comfort and ease. There is a debate about how young children should be brought up in the faith. Some say that they should not be taught anything about Christianity until they are old enough to know how to keep quiet about it at school, since there have been a number of instances of children being removed from families by social services. Others say it's better to teach children the faith, and trust God.

There are no clergy who are paid for their work, and local fellowships are pastored by men and women who make a living from various trades, as most professions are barred to Christians. There are some accountants, doctors, lawyers, and teachers who have had to keep their faith secret their entire life, and Christians are divided on whether these should be considered for church leadership roles or not. Some men act as apostles or bishops—that is, they are responsible for looking after a number of pastors and congregations over a wide area. These are usually full time and they receive remuneration from the churches, although they mostly have to have some kind of 'cover' trade as they are not able to declare their church income for tax purposes.

On the other hand, there is tremendous excitement in being part of an underground movement where Christians have to trust entirely in God. Amazing answers to prayer and seeing people come to faith are encouraging, and 'seeing Christians grow in faith' does not mean observing increased intellectual understanding of the Bible or time spent in church meetings, but watching people genuinely renounce sin in their lives, sacrificially serve others, and put the kingdom of God before material comfort. Secularism has succeeded in eliminating the church from public life: it has not succeeded in abolishing faith, because God is not dead, and he is making sure that a witness to Christ remains in England.

Andrew Symes has been executive secretary of Anglican Mainstream, based in Eynsham, Oxfordshire, since 2013. Previously, after training at All Nations Christian College, he spent twelve years in South Africa as a mission partner with the Anglican evangelical agency Crosslinks, first running a lay ministry training programme in the Diocese of St Mark the Evangelist, northern Transvaal (now Limpopo Province). After being ordained in the Anglican Church in South Africa and serving a curacy in Port Elizabeth, he taught in a small Bible college and worked with pastors of churches in townships where violence, poverty and HIV were particular problems. On returning to the UK he served as priest-in-charge of a church on a council estate in Northampton whilst completing a master's degree in mission and ministry at St John's Nottingham, a Church of England theological college. He is married with two children.

II

Britain AD 2050—Christian Revival

For here have we no continuing city, but we seek one to come (Hebrews 13:14).

To contradict TS Eliot's 1920 poem, *Gerontion*, I am 'not an old man in a dry month waiting for rain.'

Certainly I am an old man. Having been born in 1964, I have just turned 86. But spiritually speaking I am not in a dry month waiting for rain because now, in the year of our Lord 2050, the waters of Christian revival are flowing over a once dry and thirsty wasteland.

When I started as an Anglican vicar in a commuter village in the north of England in 2000, with a few exceptions local churches were dwindling, particularly in the older denominations like the Church of England and the Methodists.

Secularism seemed to have the country in an unbreakable stranglehold. Hardly any of my generation—I was then in my 30s—went to church. The congregation I served was mainly elderly.

But now Christian churches all over the country are packed to the rafters and mosques have been closing.

How did this happen?

It began with Muslim prisoners in the 2020s. Significant numbers of male Muslim prisoners became Christians in British prisons over that decade. Good evangelistic material arising out of various evangelical Bible study programmes, which had made some headway in Britain in the first quarter of the century and which explained the true biblical gospel in engaging ways, played the major part in this prison evangelism. But there were also accounts of Christ appearing in visions to Muslims in jail and telling them to get hold of a Christian Bible.

The fact is that the living God poured out his Holy Spirit on these Muslim prisoners and so Bibles instead of drugs— mind-liberating truth instead of mind-numbing lies—began to fill British prisons.

Once out of prison, an army of courageous, Holy Spirit filled ex-Muslim evangelists spread the message in conurbations around the country. Significant numbers of Muslims became Christians.

During the 2030s Muslim-background evangelists began to have a significant impact on the white population, particularly amongst young people. The faith spread rapidly throughout the 2040s.

Church in 2050

The church my wife and I go to down the road from our

retirement home is overwhelmingly under 40. It has got plenty of young families with dads fully on board. Boys' Sunday football leagues are really getting clobbered now. There is a wonderful racial and cultural mix.

They don't mind an old boy like me shuffling in. They have certainly warmed to my wife. With her people skills she's become something of a matriarch. She's practically the only old lady in the house.

The church meets in a former DIY store that unfortunately for the owners went belly-up several years ago due to the loss of Sunday trade. They had become so dependent on Sunday shopping that when local people started going to church they were badly hit. The staff were re-employed in Christian businesses around about—people are kind like that these days.

How different churches are from when I was a vicar early in the century. I remember one Sunday evening no one turned up to church. When I surveyed the sea of empty pews, I couldn't help thinking of Matthew Arnold's gloomy 1867 poem, 'On Dover Beach':

> The Sea of Faith
> Was once, too, at the full, and round earth's shore
> Lay like the folds of a bright girdle furled.
> But now I only hear
> Its melancholy, long withdrawing roar,
> Retreating to the breath
> Of the night-wind, down the vast edges drear
> And naked shingles of the world.

I almost managed to demoralise myself with this image of the 'withdrawing roar' of faith audible in the silence of the empty

church on that dusky evening early in the new millennium.
But then I remembered the Word of God:

> *Although the fig tree shall not blossom, neither shall fruit be in
> the vines; the labour of the olive shall fail, and the fields shall
> yield no meat; the flock shall be cut off from the fold, and there
> shall be no herd in the stalls: Yet I will rejoice in the Lord, I
> will joy in the God of my salvation* (Habakkuk 3:17–18).

Now, the village church I retired from in the 2030s is running
four full services on a Sunday and has a thriving youth work.
Funny that. Early on in my time there, I met an old lady who
remembered the church as it was in the 1930s with two full
Sunday schools meeting at different times. When my wife
and I arrived in 2000, the Sunday school had closed down.

Weeds in the garden

But not everything is rosy in the garden spiritually these days,
it has to be said. Some of the sermons can be thin gruel in
terms of biblical content and there are practically no prayers
of confession in church services. I top up at home using the
Book of Common Prayer's General Confession, though
on your own it is not quite the same experience as having
the Absolution declared to you publicly by a minister of
the gospel:

> Almighty God, the Father of our Lord Jesus Christ, who desirest
> not the death of a sinner, but rather that he may turn from his
> wickedness and live; and hath given power and commandment to his
> Ministers, to declare and pronounce to his people, being penitent, the
> Absolution and Remission of their sins: He pardoneth and absolveth
> all them that truly repent and unfeignedly believe his holy Gospel ...

Also, I have noticed that some people appear to be coming to church for the wrong reasons. I recently met one young man who was asking me over coffee how many leading business people there were in the church. I said we had a few but there were more in the church on the other side of town. I never saw him again.

Social change

But there is no question that society is changing due to the Revival. A new Prime Minister—a Muslim convert to Christianity as a student in the 2020s—got elected in 2045. Prime Minister Ali is a good man and has just been re-elected for a second term. Unfortunately, he's being obstructed rather in the House of Lords by the elderly secularists who still pack the benches in there but Lord willing that will change. King George is a committed Christian, so together they make a good team.

The armed forces have certainly improved. During the 2020s, they suffered some embarrassing defeats due to lack of equipment and declining standards of discipline. But recently British Special Forces rescued a group of Jewish school children from an internment camp outside Paris. France is now an Islamic state and Muslim raiders had kidnapped the children from Germany. They were trying to use the children as a bargaining chip for foreign currency and had started beheading them.

I felt a surge of patriotic pride when I heard the news of the successful British action, a feeling which may have been sinful. But thank the good Lord that lives were saved—in this instance those of people whose ethnicity our Lord shared when he became incarnate.

One of the striking things about this society is the way they have taken some things from the old secular Britain and have adapted them. For example, safeguarding children and vulnerable adults: this was becoming an increasing concern in the early part of this century. That was because of the way certain evil individuals in positions of influence had exploited the permissive society prevailing in the latter part of the twentieth-century to indulge their sexual appetites.

This society is hot on safeguarding but it has extended its concern to divorce. Prime Minister Ali has introduced a law under which divorcing parents are required to undergo an assessment of the impact of their divorce on their children. That was definitely not on the agenda back in the Noughties.

The other lovely thing that has been happening is that abortion rates have been falling significantly. In the society I grew up in, many thousands of unborn children were being killed every year—on the National Health Service.

The falling abortion rates would appear to be down to two combined factors. Amongst the under 40s the belief is taking root that the unborn child is a human being made in the image of God. That means that if a young woman does become pregnant outside marriage her family and her friends offer tremendous support and she often decides to have the child.

The second factor is that among the under 40s the ethic is taking root that the expression of sexual love should be confined to the God-created institution of heterosexual marriage.

It is the case that extramarital sex, divorce, homosexuality and transgenderism are mainly practised in this society by the late middle-aged and the elderly.

My generation—back end of the post-World War II Baby Boom—are finding the Revival quite difficult. The other day I ran into a retired bishop at the bowls club, about my age. He told me that he couldn't stand all this fundamentalism. 'The whole country's gone crackers,' he said. I hadn't heard that expression for years.

He said he's thinking of emigrating to Sweden, where public religion has been banned since the 2030s; no churches, no mosques, no temples; a land of shopping malls, multiplex leisure centres, sports stadiums and perhaps the odd bowls club if he's lucky.

A text in the churchyard

As I think about the impact of the Revival on this nation, I recall an incident that had quite an effect on me when I was visiting my elderly parents around 35 years ago in south London. A chap called Tony Corkoran was Prime Minister at the time, I seem to remember. He'd just introduced same-sex marriage and it seemed to be becoming ever more socially unacceptable to uphold orthodox Christian convictions.

It was a depressing time and I remember walking past the church we used occasionally to attend when I was a boy. On a whim really I decided to have a read of the inscriptions on the gravestones in the churchyard. I noticed one for a young man who had died in his 20s in the 1820s. His inscription included a text from the New Testament letter to the Hebrews: *For here have we no continuing city, but we seek one to come.*

The rest of his inscription made clear that he had been a committed Christian, presumably converted in the wake of the eighteenth-century Evangelical Revival. So, unless he had died suddenly without leaving any instructions—very unlikely surely in that society?—this biblical text would almost certainly have been the choice of the young man himself.

I thought to myself: how many young people these days would want a New Testament text like that on their gravestones?

That was in around 2015. Well, only the other day I saw a New Testament text on the gravestone of a recently deceased young man. He had wanted to give thanks to *the Son of God, who loved me and gave himself for me* (from Galatians 2:20).

Pleasant retirement

Yes, these are very different days from most of my Christian life. And I am enjoying quite a pleasant retirement. I've got a shed round the back with a live-stream to the cricket. I can watch old black and white films—Trevor Howard, Gary Cooper, Margaret Rutherford. I can sing along to Bob Dylan:

Seen the arrow on the doorpost
Saying, 'This land is condemned
All the way from New Orleans
To Jerusalem'
I traveled through East Texas
Where many martyrs fell
And I know no one can sing the blues
Like Blind Willie McTell ...

Well, God is in His heaven
And we all want what's his
But power and greed and corruptible seed
Seem to be all that there is
I'm gazing out the window
Of the St. James Hotel
And I know no one can sing the blues
Like Blind Willie McTell.[1]

One of the neighbours said she thought there might have been a distressed cat stuck in my shed one evening. I thought I'd better come clean.

I also like to sing along to traditional hymns, which I don't get a chance to sing in church:

Sometimes they strew His way,
And His sweet praises sing;
Resounding all the day
Hosannas to their King.
Then: 'Crucify!' is all their breath,
And for His death
They thirst and cry.[2]

On the culinary front, I can cook up spaghetti Bolognese and chilli con carne for the Bible study group. I have to admit I try to avoid DIY.

Certainly, my circumstances are very different from those the Apostle Paul had to endure in his old age—awaiting execution in that dank dungeon in Rome under the Emperor Nero in around AD 68.

---

1 From Blind Willie McTell, The Bootleg Series, Vol 1–3, Rare and Unreleased 1961–1991 (1991).
2 From 'My Song is love unknown,' Samuel Crossman, 1664.

Memory from late 1984

Contemplating this pleasant retirement, I remember an incident in late 1984 when I was an undergraduate at Cambridge University. The editor of the student newspaper, knowing that I had some connection with the Christian Union, asked me to interview the Romanian Lutheran pastor Richard Wurmbrand (1909–2001). After the Stalinist take-over of Eastern Europe at the end of World War II, he and his wife, Sabina, had suffered terribly at the hands of the Communists and he had written a celebrated book about his experiences in prison—*Tortured for Christ* (1967). In 1964 a group of Norwegian Christians had paid a ransom to the Romanian government for his release and thus the Wurmbrands came to the West as campaigners for religious freedom.[1]

They had come to Cambridge for a speaking engagement and were staying in a cheap hotel on the outskirts of the town. So, I cycled out there on a cold evening in search of a scoop.

In the hotel lounge, the Wurmbrands exuded empathy for the impertinent young man firing questions at them. After a while, Pastor Wurmbrand took control of the interview by asking me whether I was a Christian. I said that I was—a bit tentatively because I had been trying to pass myself off as a newshound. Then he really threw me, suggesting to a typical social product of 1970s London suburbia that I might one day die for my faith.

It was a transformative encounter—journalism was never

---

[1]   From Richard Wurmbrand's obituary in *The Daily Telegraph*: http://www.telegraph.co.uk/news/obituaries/1323729/Richard-Wurmbrand.html

going to be my primary calling after that—but, nearly 70 years later, a non-violent death at home or in a hospice would appear to be the most likely way my swift sparrow's flight is going to end.[1]

No continuing city

Yet still I can't get that churchyard text out of my mind—*here have we no continuing city, but we seek one to come*. In the context of the letter to the Hebrews, this statement formed part of an exhortation to a community of Christian people who were apparently being tempted to revert to some kind of Old Testament religion. The unnamed writer encouraged them to stay in the New Testament, which perfectly fulfilled the Old, and not to abandon their Christian hope, their hope of entering the eternal kingdom of the living God, the continuing city that was to come. This hope, according to the writer, was firmly grounded on the finished sin-bearing work of the Lord Jesus Christ on the cross.

Earlier on in his letter, the writer had summarised the spiritual connection in God's plan of salvation between Christ's death for sins and this New Testament hope: *And just as it is appointed for men to die once, and after that comes judgment, so Christ, having been offered once to bear the sins of many, will appear a second time, not to deal with sin but to save those who are eagerly waiting for him* (Hebrews 9:27–28 RSV).

The truth is, revival or no revival, together with his redeemed people I am looking forward to seeing the Lord

---

[1]   The old man is alluding to the analogy in Bede's eighth-century AD *Ecclesiastical History of the English People* between a person's earthly life and a sparrow's swift flight through a Saxon banqueting-hall.

and hearing from his own lips the words I first believed back
in 1983: 'Your sins have been forgiven.'

Acknowledgements:

For supporting the sabbatical from parochial duties that enabled me to write this book, thanks to the Bishop of Doncaster, the Rt Revd. Peter Burrows, and to the Revd. Dr Bill Goodman, director of ongoing ministerial development for the Diocese of Sheffield.

Thanks to those faithful ministers of the gospel who covered services at the Parish Church of the Ascension, Oughtibridge during my absence—Andy Fearnley, Andrew White, Ben Wilkinson, George Parsons, Jim Crossley, John Hutchison, and Tim Houghton.

Thanks to the Christian people in the Ascension church family for their support, including our superb churchwarden Roy Womack, Amanda Lant, Carol Simpson, Cathrine Sawdon, Claire Hennessey, David and Helen Porteous, Doreen Brooke, Geoff and Beryl Hanson, Helen Hayward, and Simon and Denise Balfour; and to Helen Kean, Lynsey Frost, Ray Martin, the Sunday Club and the Ascenders for their ministry at the family services in June and July. Without the love and prayer of the church family, this book would not have been written.

For spiritual input during the sabbatical, my thanks go to Ian Gilmour, Jonathan Milton-Thompson at the Keswick

Convention, and Mike Neville; to Oak Hill Theological College for the brilliant summer school on resilience in ministry; to the 'Old Oaks' class of 1995/96 prayer network, which has been going now for 21 years—John Shepherd, David Williams, Mike Kendall, and Tim Houghton; to the churches in Re*New* South Yorkshire whose Sunday services I attended; and to Christopher Ash for his beautiful book on the Psalms (*Teaching Psalms, Volume One—From text to message*, Proclamation Trust Resources/Christian Focus, 2017).

Finally, thanks to my parents for their hospitality at the end of the sabbatical; to Michael Magarian QC for drawing my attention to the poetic merits of *Blind Willie McTell*; to the Christian Institute for supplying me with their annual reviews from 2001; to Peter Hitchens and Andrew Symes for their interviews; and to my publisher Graham Hind of Evangelical Press. Any mistakes and shortcomings are mine.

Julian Mann is vicar of the Parish Church of the Ascension, Oughtibridge in South Yorkshire. Before ordination he was a reporter for Retail Week, *a newspaper for the directors and senior managers of retail companies. In 1993 he was EMAP Business Journalist of the Year. He is married with four sons.*